LISIEUX'S POET LAUREATE

LISIEUX'S POET LAUREATE

Gems from Saint Thérèse's Correspondence

—◊—

W. BRUCE INGRAM

Charleston, SC
www.PalmettoPublishing.com

Lisieux's Poet Laureate
Copyright © 2021 by W. Bruce Ingram
Photographs: © Archives du Carmel de Lisieux. Used with permission.

First Edition

Hardcover ISBN: 978-1-63837-884-6
Paperback ISBN: 978-1-63837-885-3
eBook ISBN: 978-1-63837-886-0

DEDICATION

This book is affectionately dedicated
to my dear mother, Rosaria Rose,
who taught me by her faith and example
the true meaning of unconditional love.

TABLE OF CONTENTS

INTRODUCTION   xi
ORGANIZATIONAL STRUCTURE   xviii

1   **LOUIS MARTIN**   **1**
    MY INCOMPARABLE KING   *4*

2   **PAULINE MARTIN**   **7**
    MATERNAL INTERCESSION   *15*
    THE EUCHARISTIC JESUS   *16*
    IN GOD'S GOOD TIME   *18*
    NO PAIN, NO GAIN   *20*
    INDIVISIBLE   *22*
    ETERNAL ESPOUSALS   *23*
    STRING OF PEARLS   *24*
    HOMEWARD BOUND   *25*
    DREAM WHISPERER   *27*
    TWENTY-FOURTH FLOOR, GOING UP   *29*
    THE TIME IS AT HAND   *30*

3   **MARIE MARTIN**   **33**
    WHEN ALL IS SAID AND DONE   *37*
    LIKE MOTHER, LIKE DAUGHTER   *38*
    KNOCK, KNOCK   *40*
    IN ANTICIPATION   *42*
    SOJOURN   *44*
    THEOLOGY 101   *46*
    PRICELESS   *48*

4   **CÉLINE MARTIN**   **50**
    SISTERS TWICE OVER   *61*
    SEPARATION ANXIETY   *63*
    A MOMENT BETWEEN TWO ETERNITIES   *64*

CONTEMPLATING IMMENSITY   66
A MARTIN ORIGINAL   68
A FAITHFUL ECHO   69
SPIRITUAL TWINSHIP   71
STALLED   73
MIDDAY   75
NOT AS THE WORLD GIVES   76
JESUS' PREDILECTION   78
RESCUED AT SEA   80
THE MARRIAGE CONTRACT   82
CROSSING THE FINISH LINE   84

5   LÉONIE MARTIN   86
     JESUS-VICTIM, YOUR SPOUSE AND MINE   89
     TRUE DEVOTEE   91

6   MARIE GUÉRIN   94
     JUXTAPOSITION   96
     LOVE ALWAYS WINS   98

7   CÉLINE GUÉRIN   101
     RSVP   103
     MATERNAL SURROGATE   104

8   ISIDORE GUÉRIN   107
     HITHER AND YON   109
     SWAN SONG   111
     FAMILIAL GRATITUDE   113

9   MARIE DE GONZAGUE   116
     THE CROSS IS OUR LOT   118

10   MARIE OF THE ANGELS   120
     RETURN TO SENDER   122

11 **MARIE OF THE TRINITY** **125**
SPIRITUAL DIRECTION *127*

12 **ALMIRE PICHON** **129**
LITTLE TOY OF JESUS *131*
THE MASTER'S HERITAGE *133*

13 **MAURICE BELLIÈRE** **136**
THE HIDDEN MANNA TO THE VICTOR *138*
THE BREEZE FROM THE CARMEL *140*

14 **ADOLPHE ROULLAND** **143**
APOSTOLIC UNION IN
THE HEART OF CHINA *144*
THE SOUL OF A MISSIONARY *146*

APPENDICES 149
APPENDIX A: THE POEMS
BY HISTORICAL PERIOD(S) 151
APPENDIX B: THE POEMS:
VERSE ATTRIBUTION BY LETTER 153
NOTES 205
SOURCES 215

INTRODUCTION

The year was 1974. I was, in more ways than I care to detail, a sophomore at Northeast Catholic High School for Boys, located in Philadelphia, Pennsylvania. The school (now closed) was situated in a predominantly blue-collar neighborhood. With few exceptions, my classmates were of the athletically oriented, rough-and-tumble, street-smart variety. I, on the other hand, was cut from the more humanities-driven, theatrically inclined cloth. In short, I was an anomaly. And—thankfully in retrospect—too inept to feign a bravado that suggested otherwise.

During my time at "North," this stark disparity with my fellow "Falcons" was never more evident, if somewhat mortifying, than in the conception and execution of a seemingly innocuous composition assignment. Dutifully compliant with having his students master the art of rhetorical persuasion, our English teacher had us write an essay comparing and contrasting our school with one of the many others in the immediate vicinity. On the due date, he went up and down the aisles, asking each student which school he had chosen for the topic and why. Invariably, irrespective of the school cited, football, baseball, wrestling, track and field, and other likeminded sports topped the list, touting wins and justifying losses, respectively. And then came my turn. Sheepishly, I announced my choice: Little Flower Catholic High School for Girls. The uproarious laughter erupted spontaneously; the louder it got, the more red-faced and self-conscious I became. When, after what seemed like an eternity, the heckling subsided, I was politely asked to stand and read my essay aloud. I sensed—indeed, truly hoped—that this teacher believed I had something worthwhile to say and that he wanted to use this unanticipated incident as a "teachable moment."

With great trepidation I cleared my throat and, amid some audible snickers and sneers, began to read. After stating some obvious facts—most notably, that Little Flower was our sister school—my commentary took a decidedly theological turn, describing the history and charism of the school named in honor of Saint Thérèse of Lisieux, as well as the Salesian character of our own school, steeped in and staffed by the Oblates of Saint Francis de Sales. By the time I finished reading my essay, the boisterous naysayers were quelled—perhaps due to boredom, though I'd like to think otherwise. At any rate, I remember the teacher congratulating me (and chiding my classmates for not being more open-minded), stating that "diverse interests make for a well-rounded education" (or something to that effect). Such was my initial foray into the life and spiritual genius of Marie Françoise-Thérèse Martin, whom Pope Saint Pius X called "the greatest saint of modern times."

Fast forward to 1986. En route to professing vows as an aspiring Augustinian, I was stationed in Racine, Wisconsin for my canonical novitiate year. The director of this program, an exceptionally devout and self-effacing man, was of the opinion that religious formation in part required exposure to the spiritual classics. And so, one after another, we were weaned on a steady diet of these literary masterpieces. While I voraciously devoured each, gleaning countless tidbits of wisdom and insight along the way, none more captivated my heart than Saint Thérèse's autobiography, *Story of a Soul*. I read and reread it many times over, always finding some new kernel of truth that had previously eluded me. This remains the case unto the present. Though my time with the Augustinians was short-lived, lasting only four years, my love affair with Saint Thérèse's love of "Love Itself" perdures.

Since my late twenties, Thérèse has been my steady support and spiritual guide. Her intercession has been invaluable in fortifying and sustaining my faith. In my view, she epitomizes—indeed, systemically embodies—a total love of and belief in God that no superlative can adequately describe. Would that I could imbibe her complete self-abandonment to God's will and her unconditional desire that He take possession of her soul. In seeking to illuminate her many secrets, I have amassed a library of biographies and treatises on her spiritual doctrine. All have been meritorious in one way or another. However, for quite some time, it has been my dream—a bucket list goal, as it were—to contribute firsthand to this already voluminous collection. But how? How could I substantively enhance the corpus of Theresian literature? Much like Thérèse's "totally new" analogy of an elevator that would raise her to Jesus, I too needed an avant-garde approach.

Enter "found poetry." A potent and evocative genre, "found poetry has a long history of practice in poetry as the imaginative appropriation and reconstruction of already-existing texts."[1] Succinctly defined as "the literary equivalent of a collage," found poetry "consists exclusively of outside texts: the words of the poem remain as they were found, with few additions or omissions. Decisions of form, such as where to break a line, are left to the poet."[2] This architectural shape shifting yields a distinctly gestalt outcome in which the newly configured whole is greater than the sum of its piecemeal parts. The distilled message of the renovated structure infuses creative energy into its original form and often exudes a purpose or function that was heretofore dormant. The legitimacy of this linguistic technique stands on solid ground.

Examples of found poems can be seen in the work of
Blaise Cendrars, David Antin, and Charles Reznikoff...
Many poets have also chosen to incorporate snippets of
found texts into larger poems, most significantly Ezra
Pound. His *Cantos* includes letters written by presidents
and popes, as well as an array of official documents
from governments and banks. *The Waste Land*, by T. S.
Eliot, uses many different texts, including Wagnerian
opera, Shakespearian theatre, and Greek mythology.
Other poets who combined found elements with their
poetry are William Carlos Williams, Charles Olson,
and Louis Zukofsky.[3]

To my knowledge, the medium of found poetry has never
been applied to the vast output of Theresian scholarship. And
while her celebrated opus, *Story of a Soul*, as well as her "pious
recreations" (plays) and poems, could well serve as goldmines
to excavate many a poetic sentiment, this book seeks to un-
earth but a few of the many "edifying thoughts"[4] contained
exclusively in her correspondence—by which I mean both the
letters she wrote and received. Regarding the latter, "we can
learn something about the characters and spiritual ideals"[5] of
the few people with whom she shared her life and vision. As
for Thérèse, we can better ascertain "her spiritual development
from childhood to death."[6] Furthermore, we must remember
that she is both a canonized Saint and an esteemed Doctor
of the Church. Thus, as historian and Theresian scholar Abbe
Andre Combes so emphatically asserts, "the least word written
by her hand is a relic."[7] Moreover, especially insofar as her let-
ters are concerned, he insists that "nothing is trite," not even

the superficial "banalities" of life that she occasionally references. These too are capable of inspiring and consoling the most humble.[8]

The letters, then, taken as a whole, are a treasure trove of precious gems from which we are capable of "drawing out suitable lessons."[9] Which is precisely my objective. Perhaps this collection of fifty-one found poems—abridged facets of affectionate exchanges—will act as a gateway, a catalyst, prompting a more in-depth study of and prayerful reflection on the doctrine of Thérèse's "Little Way." To the extent that we energize ourselves along these lines, we can, like Thérèse, be commensurately "transformed by the Spirit"[10] and share in her "mission of making God loved as I love Him."[11]

Like the content of Thérèse's own poems, the found poems contained herein focus more on substance than poetic form.[12] For Thérèse, this was by design, not happenstance—at least as attested to by Sister Marie of the Trinity who, upon entering the Carmelite Monastery at Lisieux, brought with her and later presented to Thérèse a book on the then acceptable rules of versification. After quickly thumbing through it, Thérèse repudiated it, claiming, "My poems are an outpouring from the heart, an inspiration I wouldn't know how to subject to a work of the intellect, to study. If it cost me that, I'd prefer to give up writing poetry."[13] Most of Thérèse's poems, it should be noted, were "written on request"[14] and "out of duty"[15] to both charm and encourage her "Sisters' desires."[16] To this extent—and beyond—her poems are "simple, fresh, and pure."[17] As for myself, I too would like to retain these qualities and refrain from getting bogged down in the strict adherence to poetic conventions. Moreover, in lifting and reconfiguring the words of Thérèse and her correspondents, I want to be faithful to their "vocabulary, style, and message,"[18] and thus achieve an aesthetic in which "the poetic material is sublimated by spiritual intensity."[19]

I prefer not to know all those rules;
my poems are an outpouring from the heart,
an inspiration I wouldn't know how to
subject to a work of the intellect, to study.
If it cost me that, I'd prefer to give up writing poetry.

Saint Thérèse of Lisieux

ORGANIZATIONAL STRUCTURE

The chapters of this book profile Thérèse's primary correspondents (while substantial, this list is not exhaustive). Each begins with a biographical sketch designed to provide both information and context and to highlight Thérèse's connection to and rapport with the individual in question. The (letter based) found poems then accompany the corresponding bio; their tactical arrangement is predicated on 1) the chronological timeline established in the *General Correspondence, Volumes I and II*, translated by John Clarke, O.C.D. (cited below); and 2) the dialogue between sender and recipient (i.e., who initiated the correspondence and what, if any, was the response). This will enable the reader to better gauge "the development of [Thérèse's] thought in its evolution,"[1] as spurred on and amplified by her correspondents.

The historical stages of Thérèse's life are identified as follows:

First Period: Childhood (April 1877–November 1886)
Second Period: Adolescence (Christmas 1886–April 1888)
Third Period: The Postulancy (April 9, 1888–January 10, 1889)
Fourth Period: The Novitiate (January 1889–September 1890)
Fifth Period: Novitiate: The Hidden Years (September 1890–February 1893)
Sixth Period: The Priorate of Mother Agnes of Jesus (February 1893–March 1896)
Seventh Period: The New Priorate of Mother Marie de Gonzague (March 21,1896–September 30, 1897) [2]

The period(s) from which each of the found poems originated is detailed in Appendix A.

In relation to each other and as isolated for discussion in this book, Thérèse's correspondents fall into four categories: her immediate family, her Carmelite family, her confessor/adviser, and her spiritual brothers. Apart from her biological sisters, the chapter layout is relatively straightforward and linear (as itemized in the Table of Contents). But regarding her sisters, the decision is not as clear cut. Should they be ordered by age? By maturity? By impact on Thérèse? By luck of the draw? I'm not necessarily sure that any one of these arbitrary choices is better than the others. Each, of course, would level its own criticism, perhaps like the additional one I've chosen instead (though this seems the most benign): the date of their entrance into religious life. Thus, I begin with Pauline and end with Léonie, leaving Marie and Céline sandwiched in between.

For those readers unfamiliar with Thérèse's background, the biographies, taken collectively, will more than suffice to fill in the gaps. This is not to suggest, however, that they need be read in one fell swoop. A hodgepodge approach may be just as effective since each bio stands independently as a case study in its own right. Pick and choose at random. This strategy is especially useful for the purpose of prayer and contemplation. Under the umbrella of each bio—the reading of which is a prerequisite for understanding and appreciating the nature and degree of intimacy between Thérèse and the correspondent—individual poems may well provide the impetus for experiencing, as Thérèse so movingly states, "an aspiration of the heart...a simple glance directed to heaven...a cry of gratitude and love in the midst of trial as well as joy, [and]...something great and supernatural, which expands [the] soul and unites [it] to Jesus."[3]

Readers should note well the following caveats that might otherwise be mistaken for oversights or irregularities in narrative consistency.

- The absence of letters (and thus a found poem) from Louis Martin, Thérèse's father, is threefold: 1) "He never liked writing letters"[4]; 2) His weekly visits to the Carmel "dispensed him from any writing communication"[5]; and 3) "From 1889, his mental state made all writing impossible for him right up until his death in 1894."[6]

- The *General Correspondence* references only two letters from the hand of Thérèse to Mother Marie de Gonzague. The first was written in late 1882, when Thérèse was all of nine years old. In my opinion, its content, while innocent and endearing, is entirely too sparse to assume the stature of a found poem. The second entry, written in June 1896, took the form of a parable aimed at fortifying Mother de Gonzague's confidence in once again undertaking the Office of Prioress, due to her intuition that some members of the community "seemed to be traitors to her."[7] In view of its symbolic substance and intended purpose, I felt it unwise to mar the integrity of its original content—hence, the absence of a found poem from Thérèse to Mother Marie de Gonzague.

- Two remaining aberrations require explanation: 1) The complete nonexistence of Thérèse's letters to Sister Marie of the Angels and Father Almire Pichon, both of whom later testified at the diocesan tribunal that they destroyed her correspondence "because they did not suspect at the time their real value"[8] ; and 2) The conspicuous lack of any correspondence on the part of Sister Marie of the Trinity, Thérèse's youngest novice "and her most ardent disciple."[9] While there is evidence to suggest that she did indeed pen some missives to Thérèse, these unfortunately have been lost. Consequently, the complementary arrangement of found poems for these individuals has been waived out of necessity.

Louis Martin

1

LOUIS MARTIN
(1823–1894)

Louis Martin was the venerable patriarch of nine children. But, given the high infant mortality rate in nineteenth-century Europe, only five—all girls—survived to adulthood. Even more than providing tangible and financial security for his children, Louis was adamantly determined to instill in them a knowledge of and fidelity to the precepts and traditions of the Catholic faith. He "sought no worldly disposition for his daughters… but wished they would all dedicate themselves to God."[1] His beloved wife, Zélie, was of a decidedly likeminded persuasion. In fact, before their marriage, both had unsuccessfully attempted to enter monastic orders. In many respects, then, "the children were all raised unequivocally to view the convent as their destiny."[2] And so it came to pass. All the Martin girls eventually professed vows as consecrated religious and lived the remainder of their lives in cloistered settings.

After the untimely death of Zélie at age forty-five to breast cancer, Louis moved his family from Alençon to Lisieux "so that Zélie's last wish could be fulfilled."[3] There, his daughters could complete their formative years under the watchful eyes of Isidore and Céline Guérin, Zélie's brother and sister-in-law, the former having been named "the surrogate guardian of his five nieces."[4] Situated at the town's center was the Carmelite monastery. In 1882, Pauline, Louis' second oldest, would be the first to enter this convent at the age of twenty-one; four years later, Marie, the first born, followed in her footsteps at the age of twenty-six.

Realistically, Louis could not have been too terribly surprised to learn that his youngest, Thérèse, harbored similar inclinations, though the timing of her decision certainly caught him off guard. Despite being taken aback and perhaps secretly crestfallen at the prospect of his little queen's departure at the tender age of only fifteen, he refused to subvert her will and to undermine the authenticity of her vocation. Rather, he stood by her side and staunchly defended her cause against the many obstacles she faced in pursuit of her entrance to Carmel, even to the point of taking her to Rome to solicit Pope Leo XIII's approval. In the end, her persistence and numerous appeals finally triumphed. With ethereal elation, Thérèse entered the Lisieux Carmel on April 9, 1888. She described this momentous event, indelibly etched into her psyche, in all but celestial terms: "My desires were at last accomplished; my soul experienced a PEACE so sweet, so deep, it would be impossible to express it…I was fully recompensed for all my trials. With what deep joy I repeated those words: 'I am here forever and ever!'"[5]

Among the many hardships Thérèse endured behind the walls of Carmel was the illness and eventual death of her "incomparable king." A month after her Reception of the Habit on January 10, 1889, Louis suffered a cerebral hemorrhage. Over the course of the next five years—culminating in his death on July 29, 1894—Thérèse and her sisters "knew him only as a living corpse, first among strangers in an institution, then at home under the care of Léonie and Céline."[6] Well in advance of the inevitable, Céline openly acknowledged her own aspirations for a life in Carmel but put these on hold to care for the needs of her dying father. Less than two months after his death, Céline's desires came to fruition as "the doors of the holy ark"[7] closed upon her. As for Léonie, after three aborted attempts to join religious life, she definitively entered the Visitation Monastery at Caen in January of 1899.

Indisputably, according to Dorothy Day, "Louis Martin's vocation was a great one, although he was not to spend his days in the religious life or in a struggle to better social conditions. It was through marriage and the bringing up of a family that he was to play his great and saintly role in the world."[8] This appraisal was affirmed by many ecclesiastical authorities, not the least of whom was Pope Francis, who, on October 18, 2015, officially proclaimed both Louis Martin and his devoted wife, Zélie, saints of the Roman Catholic Church.

MY INCOMPARABLE KING

[Adapted From the Letters of Thérèse to Louis Martin]

In the nest of Carmel, I have found my way.
When taking me for Himself from under the
Cart, Jesus, the King of Heaven, has not taken
Me away from my holy King on earth; always I
Shall remain Papa's Queen of France and Navarre.

You as both a Father and a King wanted to entrust
The little blond rascal only to the King of Heaven.
You could not do more for your little Queen; and
From the Orpheline de la Bérésina I passed to the
Very noble title of Carmelite.

Except to see my dear King entirely cured, I no
Longer desire anything whatsoever on earth.
God always tries those whom He loves; and
I cannot believe there's anyone whom God
Loves more than my dear little Father!

God wills to give my King a magnificent throne, so
Beautiful and elevated above all human thoughts.
Your Queen too would like to give her King the
Immense treasures of infinite horizons, but Jesus
Alone possesses these.

Your Queen rejoices thinking of the day when she
Will reign with you in the true kingdom of heaven.
Soon the day without shadows will light up for us,
And then never will we end our conversation.
Ah, what God reserves for those whom He loves!

The Queen will do her best to resemble her King.
She will try to be his glory by becoming a great saint.
May Jesus grant you, Papa, His blessings and give you
The hundredfold in this life and heaven in the next.
This is the wish of your little Queen!

Pauline Martin

2

PAULINE MARTIN
(1861–1951)

The second-born daughter of Louis and Zélie Martin, Pauline was undeniably her mother's favorite. "Zélie confessed to her sister that in her prayers she had described to the Blessed Mother just the kind of child she would like, 'dotting the i's and crossing the t's.' And she claimed that in Pauline she got just what she wanted."[1] Even more than a daughter, Zélie viewed Pauline as her adult equal and counselor of sorts, writing to her at the age of fifteen, "You are a true friend to me; you give me courage to endure life with patience."[2] Not merely by her mother but by virtually all, Pauline was considered "lively and ardent in temperament, and sensible beyond her years."[3]

Still reeling from the deathblow of Zélie, Pauline and her older sister Marie were charged with the task of raising their younger sisters—Thérèse in particular, as she was only four and a half at the time. Upon Zélie's death, Thérèse chose Pauline as her second mother. "Pauline represented for Thérèse, according to her own admission, 'a child's ideal.' Instinctively, every child chooses a model that he or she tries to copy exactly. Thérèse's model was Pauline...for she was incomparable, gifted in everything."[4] Pauline was especially adept at solidifying in Thérèse her penchant for all things spiritual. Without question, Pauline "represented the strongest guiding and shaping element in Thérèse's growth."[5] Thérèse herself was quite cognizant of this and acknowledged as much in her autobiography: "With so much love and tenderness…you brought the most sublime mysteries down to my level of understanding and were able to give my soul the nourishment it needed."[6]

Perhaps the single most—almost inexcusable—faux pas regarding Pauline's otherwise conscientious guardianship of Thérèse was her failure to exercise due diligence in preparing Thérèse for her departure to the Lisieux Carmel. Upon overhearing Pauline divulge her decision to Marie, Thérèse was shaken to the core, experiencing yet again the existential angst of maternal abandonment. Later, Thérèse recalled this traumatizing event with these heartrending words: "I was about to lose my second Mother! Ah! how can I express the anguish of my heart! In one instant, I understood what life was; until then, I had never seen it so sad; but it appeared to me in all its reality, and I saw it was nothing but a continual suffering and separation. I shed bitter tears because I did not yet understand the joy of sacrifice."[7]

Pauline (Sister/Mother Agnes of Jesus) entered the Carmelite monastery on October 2, 1882, at the age of twenty-one; Thérèse at the time was only nine years old. In the months that followed, bereft of consolation, Thérèse became critically ill, suffering from a myriad of inexplicable symptoms, including convulsive seizures, incessant headaches, violent tremors, vivid hallucinations, terrifying nightmares, episodic amnesia, and paranoid delusions. A somewhat laissez-faire attitude regarding medical intervention, coupled with an acute "attack of unprecedented violence,"[8] compelled Marie and her sister Léonie to fall to their knees and pray to the statue of the Blessed Mother—*The Virgin of the Smile*—stationed in Thérèse's room. "And Thérèse, too…fixed her wild eyes upon the statue and inwardly joined passionately in their prayers."[9] Within a matter of moments, "Marie saw the child's eyes clear, wholly tranquil, blissfully radiant; Thérèse recognized her at once and smiled at her in the midst of tears. Thérèse was cured. The very next day, she resumed ordinary life."[10]

The miraculous nature of this cure notwithstanding, the pain associated with human exile persisted. In the absence of Pauline, Thérèse was cared for by her oldest sister, Marie; but now she too decided to take flight and join Pauline in the convent. Thérèse was thrice abandoned. By this point, however, she was nearly fourteen and on the verge of making her own commitment to a life of religious consecration. When Marie (Sister Marie of the Sacred Heart) learned that Thérèse was determined to enter Carmel at the age of fifteen, she was adamantly opposed on the grounds that she was entirely too young to make such a life-altering decision. But, for her part, Pauline more than openly supported and encouraged Thérèse; she in fact did everything in her power to accommodate Thérèse's quest. First and foremost, Pauline recognized that this was not a whim but rather a long-sought-after dream—articulated by Thérèse since the age of nine—coming to fruition. Moreover, "Pauline believed sincerely in the idea of vocation, the 'call' from God. For a woman to cut herself off from the ordinary pleasures of life, to drape her body in thick dark wool, and devote her day to prayer, to work, to fasting in the stark cloister made sense only if one had a vocation, and Pauline believed that Thérèse had such a call."[11]

Aware of the many stumbling blocks Thérèse would have to confront—not the least of which included convincing her deputy guardian, Uncle Guérin, and procuring the permission of ecclesiastical authorities—Pauline was nevertheless determined to help Thérèse brave the elements and navigate her ship safely to port. After a well-fought valiant effort—and the grace of God—including an appeal to Pope Leo XIII, Thérèse arrived at her destination. Once inside, her mission and mystical genius were meteoric in their ascension. Thérèse (Sister Thérèse of the Child Jesus and the Holy Face) could not have been more delighted: "With what deep joy I repeated those words: 'I am here forever and ever!' This happiness was not passing. It didn't take its flight with 'the illusions of the first days.' Illusions, God gave me the grace not to have A SINGLE ONE when entering Carmel. I found the religious life to be exactly as I had imagined it."[12]

While Thérèse was more than willing to embrace the "thorns" associated with community life, Pauline expressed some serious reservations about Thérèse's mistreatment. She later lamented that Thérèse "was to be extremely neglected, and very little attention was paid to her health! I witnessed unbelievable acts of carelessness, and I was powerless to stop them."[13] As acknowledged by many of the nuns, the lion's share of the abuse heaped upon Thérèse was attributed to the Prioress, Mother Marie de Gonzague, who "was not sparing in her use of reprimands and humiliations where Sister Thérèse was concerned."[14] In her defense, however, Mother de Gonzague did not want Thérèse to become the community pet and thereby stifle her potential, which she saw as enormous.

In 1893, Pauline, at the age of thirty-one, was elected to succeed Mother de Gonzague as Prioress. Although Pauline's term of office was often fraught with chaotic scenes staged by Mother de Gonzague to upend her authority, Thérèse found her Priorate to be a source of spiritual nourishment: "O Mother, it was especially since the blessed day of your election that I have flown in the ways of love. On that day Pauline became my living Jesus."[15] In an attempt to satiate Mother de Gonzague' s thirst for power, Pauline appointed her as Mistress of Novices, but because she had some qualms about the influence she might impart on those in formation, she simultaneously selected Thérèse to serve as her assistant. Despite her age—Thérèse was only nineteen at the time—she eventually won the admiration and respect not only of her novices but of Mother de Gonzague as well. In their first year of this joint venture, Mother de Gonzague declared that Thérèse possessed "the wisdom, perfection and perspicacity of a fifty-year-old," that she was in fact "a little 'untouchable saint' to whom you would give the Good God without confession."[16]

Besides the death of their father and the subsequent entrance of their sister, Céline (Sister Geneviève of the Holy Face), and their cousin, Marie Guérin (Sister Marie of the Eucharist), to the Carmel during Pauline's Priorate, two other events changed the trajectory of Thérèse's legacy. She longed for a spiritual brother, a priest, for whom she would pray in particular, and he in return would remember her each day at the altar. Her wish was fulfilled when Pauline, in her capacity as Prioress, received a request from Maurice Bellière, a seminarian and candidate for the foreign missions, to be given "a Sister who would devote herself especially to the salvation of his soul and aid him through her prayers and sacrifices."[17] Pauline chose Thérèse to become the sister of this future missionary. This news enthralled Thérèse: "Not for years had I experienced this kind of happiness. I felt my soul was renewed; it was as if someone had struck for the first time musical strings left forgotten until then."[18] From this point forward until Thérèse's death, "they exchanged twenty-one letters, and that correspondence opens a window on the heart of St. Thérèse which would have remained forever closed if Maurice had not written to the Carmel, asking for a Sister to pray for him."[19] The second event, germane to the cult of Thérèse, involved the act of obedience under which Pauline placed Thérèse to record her childhood memories (Manuscript A). Without this directive, made at the suggestion of their sister Marie for the purpose of preserving familial intimacies, the story of Thérèse's soul would never have been told.

Having dutifully complied with Pauline's edict, Thérèse submitted her composition to her sister on January 20, 1896, the feast of Saint Agnes. At the time, however, Pauline was distracted by the machinations surrounding the upcoming election, in which she was unseated as Prioress by Mother de Gonzague. It was several months after this contentious election that Pauline finally got around to reading Thérèse's memoirs. And though she was edified by the content and caliber of what Thérèse had written, she found "her account incomplete" insofar as she "had dealt with her religious life only in barest outline."[20] But now she was no longer authorized to compel Thérèse to complete her story. It was only when Thérèse's death (from the ravages of pulmonary and intestinal tuberculosis) became imminent that Pauline suggested to Mother de Gonzague the prospect of ordering Thérèse to write about her life in Carmel, ostensibly for the purpose of gathering information that could be used in composing her obituary notice. And with that stipulation, Mother de Gonzague consented and placed Thérèse under obedience to continue writing. Thérèse, of course, obliged, resulting in the production of Manuscript C. Flanked by Manuscripts A and C was "the jewel of Thérèse's writings,"[21] Manuscript B, a letter requested by and addressed to her sister Marie, in which Thérèse proffered a sublime synopsis of her little doctrine.

Clearly, these documents were never intended for public consumption. However, as Thérèse lay dying in the infirmary, Pauline hinted to her that the publication of her manuscripts "might well be the means that God would use to realize her ambition to do good on earth after her death."[22] It was thus that, in concession to this suggestion, Thérèse authorized Pauline to act as editor of her writings: "She gave her permission to add, to delete, to make any changes necessary."[23] Thérèse believed that this would be a vehicle to help fulfill her growing "sense of mission, a feeling that she had not had her religious insights and experiences for herself and the few relatives of her own blood who were dearest to her but for many."[24]

After Thérèse's death, Pauline proposed the possibility of publishing Thérèse's manuscripts to Mother de Gonzague. She agreed but on one condition: "that all three must be rearranged in such a way as to seem to be addressed to herself."[25] With this political proviso settled, Pauline assiduously undertook the editorial work Thérèse had commissioned her to complete. Having the best of intentions, Pauline "polished" Thérèse's notebooks "with the zeal of a schoolmistress, in order to make sure that they would be presented respectfully to the world."[26] Never had she sought to distort or falsify the real Thérèse from public view as some critics contended. (The subsequent unedited editions amply testify to this fact.) The changes Pauline made "do not," as she put it, "affect the substance or general meaning of the account."[27] On the one-year anniversary of Thérèse's death, September 30, 1898, two thousand copies of her collected manuscripts were published under the title *Histoire d'une Ame* (*Story of a Soul*). The public's reaction to this book was at once swift and mind boggling, igniting a spark of epic proportions. The universal appeal of Thérèse's little way was—and still remains—"an explosive force that can transform our lives and the life of the world, once put into effect."[28]

As Thérèse's fame—empirically demonstrated by sales and translations of her autobiography, the arrival of pilgrims to Lisieux, requests for relics, reports of cures and conversions, the influx of applicants to Carmel, etc.—increased exponentially, Pauline remained faithful to the promise she made to Thérèse in June of the year she died: "I shall be your little herald; I shall proclaim your feats of arms; I shall endeavor to bring others to the love and service of God through all the illuminations which He has vouchsafed to you, and which shall never pass."[29] In 1902, Pauline once again commanded the reigns as Prioress and, absent a period of eighteen months, held this post until her death in 1951. Over these many years, both she and her sisters witnessed the "storm of glory" that little Thérèse unleashed, not only on Lisieux but on the world at large. They all lived to see their sister elevated to the ranks of sainthood. And from the time of her death to their own, they devoted the remainder of their cloistered existence to promulgating the message and mission of their beloved sister. This "disposition of Providence became," according to Theresian scholar Ida Friederike Görres, "the true fulfillment of their lives."[30]

MATERNAL INTERCESSION
[Adapted From the Letters of Pauline to Thérèse]

When you were sick, all Paradise was in a flutter.
But beneath the Blessed Virgin's glance, beneath
Her hand, the little bark of her heart is now safe
And sailing peacefully toward heaven.

Mary, your mother, wants her daughter to resemble
Her and become like her, a beautiful lily of purity
And innocence; may she always watch over you and
Keep you under her virginal mantle.

Like His mother, the Child Jesus constantly looks at
His little Thérèse—He smiles at her, blesses her,
Watches over her, tenderly caresses her, and loves
Her more than the heavens.

Offer to this Child Jesus a bouquet of flowers, acts
Of virtue, gathered in the garden of gentleness.
These flowers won't fade but will be preserved by
The angels to form your heavenly crown.

THE EUCHARISTIC JESUS
[Adapted From the Letters of Pauline to Thérèse]

The day of First Communion is the most beautiful
Day in our life; it is a heavenly day!
To taste its infinite charms, we must always busily
Cultivate the little garden of our heart, turning it
Into nothing less than an angel's heart.

What nature is doing to give joy to our eyes, you
Also must do: receive and give joy to the beloved
Little Child at His first awakening in your heart.
Spare yourself nothing to make your soul a little
Heaven where Jesus will want to dwell forever.

A little heart, very innocent, very gentle, filled
With good will and the desire to please Him, what
A delightful home, what a pleasant crib for Him.
The treasures, the marvels of this little Host, the
Heart of Jesus, claiming entrance into your soul.

I see Him smiling at you from the Tabernacle.
Tell Him to come and help prepare His little girl's
Heart for the great day when the golden door of His
Amiable prison of love will finally swing open—a door
You are going to knock on a thousand times a day.

From now on place all your joy in goodness, in love
For Jesus, for we cannot be truly happy except with
This only joy; may this gentle Child already be the
King, the love of your heart.
Long live Thérèse's Jesus!

IN GOD'S GOOD TIME
[Adapted From the Letters of Thérèse to Pauline]

My little boat is having a lot of trouble reaching
Port: the blessed shore of Carmel.
There, I shall desire to suffer always for Jesus.
Suffering borne with joy can save souls.
How happy I would be to have a soul to offer
Jesus at the moment of my death.

My time of trial is about to begin, but truly a
Drop of gall must be mingled in all chalices.
Life isn't cheerful; attachment to it is difficult.
Though my heart is heavy and I feel sad and
Alone on this earth, God suffices; I will all that
He wills and want to refuse Him nothing.

I am the Child Jesus' little ball; if He wishes to
Break His toy, He is free, for He cannot give
Me trials that are above my strength.
In order that His little ball roll where He wills,
Jesus must prepare all; the last step that
Remains for me is to speak to the pope.

Of my entrance to Carmel at fifteen, the Holy
Father said simply: "If God wills it, you will enter."
It is only the world which is the obstacle, citing
Public scandal and the rules of human prudence.
But God will not be at a loss to show the world
That these obstacles don't exist.

Life passes so quickly that it must be better to
Have a very beautiful crown and a little trouble
Than to have an ordinary one without any trouble.
I am filled with courage; God will not abandon me.
Having done all He asked me to do, there is now
Nothing left for me but to pray.

NO PAIN, NO GAIN
[Adapted From the Letters of Pauline to Thérèse]

Jesus seems to be sleeping in your little boat, but
His Heart is watching; fear nothing, for Jesus says
To you as He did to St. Teresa: "Nobody will be
Able to snatch you from My Hands."

The desperate hours are always God's hours.
It is when there is no longer any hope that the
Sleeping Jesus awakens and commands as Master
The winds and the tempest.

The heart torn by thorns is a thousand times closer
To the Heart of the Jesus than the heart filled with
Joy; when it is He sending His little ball into the
Midst of thorns, the thorns will change into flowers.

He is a Spouse of blood; to resemble Him and bear
The name of Spouse worthily, you must raise your
Heart and fight the good fight in order to carry off
The victory and merit the crown.

Without the Cross, one is sure of nothing; without
The Cross, there is only the human element, the
Mundane; without the Cross, Jesus is not there.
Your vocation is marked with this sacred sign.

The bonds are already formed between Jesus and
His little Thérèse; you are the St. John of Jesus,
Always leaning on His Heart—what a privilege!
Jesus will soon pluck His little flower.

To merit the suffering of the cloister, you must gently
Endure the suffering of waiting for the divine Lamb.
Entrust to Jesus the great matter of your entrance.
It is an act of abandonment that you must make.

Prepare your soul for the mountain of Carmel.
There, you will live hidden in the Heart of Jesus.
All passes, except the love of Jesus for Thérèse
And the love of Thérèse for Jesus!

INDIVISIBLE
[Adapted From the Letters of Thérèse to Pauline]

If not through blood then through love,
The grain of sand wishes to form beautiful
Eternities for the souls of sinners.
But, alas, it is still not little or light enough.

To convert all sinners and to save all souls
In purgatory, pray Mamma that the grain
Of sand become an ATOM seen only by
The eyes of Jesus.

To give all to Jesus who alone is perfect joy…
Joy found only in suffering without consolation!
Weakness, agonies of the heart, pinpricks…
Give rise to the grain of sand's confidence.

No matter what happens to it, it wants only
To see the sweet, gentle hand of its Jesus.
Nothing is too much to suffer to gain the palm:
Jesus alone, nothing but Him!

It would be a mistake to look elsewhere for
A shadow of beauty, a shadow of happiness.
Only in eternity will the unknown grain of sand
Find Jesus and become brilliant and bright.

ETERNAL ESPOUSALS
[Adapted From the Letters of Pauline to Thérèse]

Although Jesus is saying nothing to us,
He is acting at the bottom of our heart.
This suffering brings us closer to Him
And frees us from all attachment.

Our heart cannot live without love.
But to give it life, let our heart
Love Jesus alone; every other love
Will cause it to die.

When we are united to Jesus and
Think of pleasing Him in all things,
The soul begins, in Divine silence,
The great Retreat of Eternity.

All the days in Carmel are days of
Retreat…in suffering…in the labors
Of this exile…to terminate in the
Rest without end of the homeland.

We sow in tears to reap the marvels
Of our Beloved Spouse, who will
Imprint His Divine Face on the white
Veil of our virginity forever.

STRING OF PEARLS
[Adapted From the Letters of Thérèse to Pauline]

There is no support outside of Jesus.
He alone is immutable.
He cannot change.

Jesus does not look at time.
There is no time in heaven.
He must look only at love.

Keep all for Jesus with a jealous care.
Desire to be counted for nothing.
Prefer the monotony of sacrifice.

Look at the Beloved's face only.
Catch the tears flowing from His eyes.
Dry the tears of this Spouse of blood.

Consent to walk on the dark road.
Enter a subterranean passage.
Be happy to have no consolation.

Thank Jesus for silence.
Follow the heart into solitude.
Abandon all glory to Him.

Save souls at all costs.
Climb the mountain of Love.
Contemplate Jesus eternally.

HOMEWARD BOUND
[Adapted From the Letters of Pauline to Thérèse]

Nothing bright can strike
The wounded eyes of Jesus
Without making Him suffer.
He can walk in our darkness
Without suffering too much.

On earth there can be only suffering
For those who love and seek with ardor
The gentle, suffering Face of Jesus.
Let us annihilate ourselves for Him.
Only the cowardly desire consolations.

Grace works marvels in the faithful heart.
This gives us courage: today, we are sad;
The next day, sadness vanishes; two
Days later, the sky clouds over again.
How everything passes here below!

A thousand times blessed is the soul
That lifts itself above these vicissitudes.
Jesus is pleased with its desires.
Let Him be under no constraint.
Let Him do what He wills.

After this exile of struggles and tears,
Our souls will rise to the homeland of glory.
What a blessedness to hope for:
This great Eternal Vision
Lighted by the divine Lamb.

DREAM WHISPERER
[Adapted From the Letters of Thérèse to Pauline]

The night has come; the Child Jesus falls asleep.
Dreaming, He sees in the distance a cross, a lance,
A crown of thorns; His Infant Face is disfigured,
Covered with blood, unrecognizable.

But knowing that His spouse will always recognize
Him, that she will be at His side when all others
Abandon Him, Jesus smiles at this bloodstained image,
At the chalice filled with wine giving birth to virgins.

He realizes that, in His Eucharist, the ungrateful will
Desert Him; but thinking of His spouse's love, her
Attention, her holy consecration as prioress, Jesus
Continues to sleep on peacefully.

He who is still hidden in His little white Host and who
Communicates Himself to souls only as veiled has cast
On His faithful apostle His veiled look; He does not
Allow her to be recognized, for her face too is hidden.

Becoming in her turn a Mother of many virgins, among
Whom are her own Sisters, Jesus pours out on her the
Perfume of the mysterious bouquet and imprints on her
The eternal seal of His Adorable Face.

She now penetrates the sanctuary of souls, imparting upon
Them the treasures of grace with which Jesus has filled her.
But these vessels are too little to contain the precious
Perfume she wants to place in them.

It is thus, like Jesus, that she will suffer; however, up
Above, in the celestial gardens, the angels, servants of
The divine Child, are already weaving crowns His Heart
Has reserved for His beloved.

He sees the flowers of her virtues as they scent the
Tabernacle; these will always remain hidden in His crib.
So He awaits the shadows to lengthen, the night of
Life to give way to the bright day of eternity.

Then Jesus will give back to His beloved spouse the
Flowers she had given Him, consoling Him on earth;
Then He will lower His radiant Face and allow His spouse
To taste the ineffable sweetness of His divine kiss.

TWENTY-FOURTH FLOOR, GOING UP
[Adapted From the Letters of Thérèse to Pauline]

You, my dear Mother, are the image of God's
Tenderness; you have been and always will
Be the Angel charged with leading me and
Announcing to me the mercies of the Lord!

The good you have done to my soul, you have
Done to Jesus, for He said, "What you have
Done to the least of my brethren, you have
Done to me," and I am the one who is the least!

I hope to go soon up above: heaven is for me.
There, I shall have all God's treasures, and He
Himself will be my good; then I shall be able to
Return to you a hundredfold all I owe you.

When I shall be far away from this sad earth, I
Shall be very close to the Angel whom Jesus sent
Before me to prepare the way leading to heaven,
The elevator lifting me to the infinite regions of love!

We are all flowers that God gathers in His own
Time, a little earlier, a little later; I, a short-lived
Creature, am going there the first, but we shall find
One another in Paradise and enjoy true happiness!

THE TIME IS AT HAND
[Adapted From the Letters of Pauline to Thérèse]

White dove, it is time that the Master of the dovecote
Set you in your place; it is time that the little angels
Be no longer deprived of your company; it is time that
God may receive new glory through your entrance into
The heavenly homeland.

Arise, dear dove, the winter is past for you, the fountain
Of your tears is dried up, come and taste the delights of
The eternal fountain of love; what a beautiful crown has
Been made for you, what glory you have given to God.
Ah! there will be a big to-do upon your arrival in heaven.

So strong and limitless, like the ocean, is the ebb and
Flow I feel in my heart for my dear Angel: I would like
To let you leave and, at the same time, keep you here.
I can cry only with one eye, knowing that my little Angel
Is soon going to leave this sad prison to enter into glory.

My soul escapes its frail envelope when thinking that
White and gilded wings are growing on you; they need
Only a light breeze from on high to set them in motion.
After your departure, return to embellish this world, and
With a luminous breath, make it a little sun.

Since the saints in heaven can still receive glory until the
End of time, I shall be your herald and proclaim your
Feats of arms; I shall take care to make God loved and
Served by means of all the inextinguishable lights He has
Given you, and your presence shall be felt everywhere.

Marie Martin

3

MARIE MARTIN
(1860–1940)

The firstborn of Louis and Zélie Martin, Marie was pragmatic in her outlook, stubborn in her resolutions, and independent—some would say gruff—in her behavior. She often refused, for example, to bow to persons of her acquaintance, as was customary; she rebelled against the family maid's dictates, claiming, "I am quite free,"[1] and, instead of lowering her head at the elevation of the Host during Mass, she obstinately—albeit reverently—contemplated the spectacle with wide eyes. During her formal schooling at the Convent of the Visitation, she was popular and intellectually astute, taking home many prizes and accolades for her efforts. Though "she hated being dressed up or made up,"[2] for a time she put on airs with her classmates, most of whom "belonged to the nobility."[3] This adolescent phase, induced by peer pressure, was relatively short lived. Not long after Marie left school at the age of fifteen, Zélie noted, "I am quite satisfied with Marie. The things of this world do not penetrate her heart as deeply as do spiritual things."[4]

After the death of Zélie and the subsequent entrance to Carmel of her younger sister, Pauline, Marie was charged with the day-to-day task of rearing Thérèse. She was quite masterful in this pivotal role, "a sober and sensible guardian"[5] who diligently prepared Thérèse for her First Communion, navigated with the upmost tact and decorum her battle with scruples, and, most notably, aided with piety and devotion her emotional crisis—hallucinations, seizures, paralysis—when she was ten years old. At the height of this mysterious illness, Thérèse, who no longer recognized Marie, accused her sister of trying to poison her. "Frantic, Marie knelt by a statue of the Virgin Mary and pleaded for her sister's life. She watched Thérèse 'fix her gaze on the statue,' grow calm, and begin to cry quietly. The symptoms vanished."[6] Later, Thérèse confessed, "The Blessed Virgin had appeared very beautiful, and I had seen her smile at me."[7]

Some four years after Pauline entered Carmel, Marie decided to follow in her sister's footsteps, leaving Thérèse, once again, vulnerable to feelings of abandonment. Thérèse herself admitted, "As soon as I learned of Marie's determination, I resolved to take no pleasure out of earth's attractions."[8] Although "Marie had never been her *petite mère* like Pauline…she had been 'my last support…who used to guide my soul.'"[9]

Prior to her entrance to Carmel, Marie "had a distinct disinclination towards the religious life."[10] But her confessor, Father Pichon, along with Pauline, persuaded her otherwise. "She yielded finally…simply in the belief that her confessor was proclaiming the will of God, and in her readiness to obey that will unconditionally."[11] Such blind faith and loyalty led to nearly fifty-four years behind Carmel's enclosure. During this time, Marie (Sister Marie of the Sacred Heart) held a number of offices, including assistant infirmarian, refectorian, bursar, and gardener. In an autobiographical account to Pauline (Mother Agnes of Jesus, Prioress), Marie declared, "Ah, Mother, I have found Jesus within these four walls and, in finding Him, I have found heaven! Yes, it is here that I have passed the happiest years of my life."[12]

When in her mid-teens Thérèse announced her wish to become a Carmelite, Marie was dead set against the idea. Her rationale was twofold: not only was Thérèse entirely too young, but "I feared the great grief it would be to our father, since Thérèse was the true sunshine of his life."[13] Marie's opposition joined a litany of likeminded discordant voices; they were all successfully silenced, however, enabling Thérèse to enter Carmel at the tender age of fifteen. Marie later changed her tune regarding Thérèse's readiness for religious life. In her own words, Marie unambiguously exclaimed, "What perfection in every least act, and yet, what simplicity! How many times while watching her pass through the cloister, simple, modest, recollected, have I said to myself, 'Oh, to think that no one will ever know here below how much this soul loves the good God!'"[14] On this score, Marie was categorically mistaken. Ironically, it was she who changed the course of Thérèse's worldwide acclaim by insisting that Pauline require Thérèse, under obedience, to record her childhood memories (Manuscript A); moreover, it was she who asked Thérèse to detail in writing the doctrine of her "Little Way of Spiritual Childhood" (Manuscript B). Absent these two requests, Thérèse's autobiography would never have seen the light of day.

Marie lived to witness the beatification and canonization of her beloved little sister and goddaughter. But from 1924 until her death in 1940, she suffered from rheumatism, which progressively worsened to the point of complete paralysis. "She remained ever serene," according to Pauline, "and kept the salvation of souls uppermost in mind, lamenting heroically: 'I am as one in chains. I am fettered and constrained; my arms pain me. But I offer this to the good God in order that some poor soul may not be fettered and lost for all eternity.'"[15] At two o'clock in the morning of January 19, 1940, Sister Marie of the Sacred Heart, surrounded by the members of her community, and with crucifix in hand, "gazed steadily at the statue of Our Lady of the Smile…bowed her head, and with an expression of peace and joy on her face…expired."[16]

WHEN ALL IS SAID AND DONE
[Adapted From the Letters of Marie to Thérèse]

At the feet of the Holy Father as upon Jesus
Himself, you opened your heart and He blessed
You, saying: "You will enter if God wills it."

These words from heaven are enveloped in
Mystery, filled with light and the special love
Of Jesus; never forget this remarkable grace.

At the hour, at the minute He wills it, you will
Enter His own house, and He will not be
Hampered in the least opening the doors.

Never grow weary of being the ball of Jesus.
Don't roll one single instant far from His cradle.
Approach it and remain there always.

Jesus has marked you as His spouse with the sign
Of the Cross; but what sweet things He is hiding
From you: under this Cross, there are only roses.

Yes, dear child, you can say in all truth as the virgin
Agnes said: "He has set His seal on my forehead!"
Jesus does not leave you for the space of a step.

You would not be His privileged one if you never
Brought your lips to His bitter chalice; so hope
Always, for God reserves the last word to Himself.

LIKE MOTHER, LIKE DAUGHTER
[Adapted From the Letters of Thérèse to Marie]

The Hermit of the Heart of Jesus,
An eagle called to soar the heights,
To fix its gaze on the Sun,
Possesses strength and courage
To surmount all things.

The little toy of Jesus would like
To resemble this eagle-angel,
But it is weakness itself.
If He does not throw His little ball,
It will remain inert.

The toy-daughter implores
Its hermit-mother to pray that
She may be reduced to nothing,
Content to remain a grain of sand
Recognized only by Jesus.

To the Heart of Him who alone
Reads into the depths of the soul,
May she, filled with sacrifices, a
Feeble reed at the bottom of the valley,
Love Jesus without reserve!

Only in the homeland will the heart's
Burning thirst for joy be quenched.
To arrive there, to drink from this Spring,
The eagle and the toy must remain
Unknown, hidden for Jesus alone to see!

KNOCK, KNOCK
[Adapted From the Letters of Marie to Thérèse]

Here below, nothing can satisfy the
Hunger of the lion or the little lamb;
Here below, the Cross; here below,
The exile, the arid desert.

Never shall we suffer as much as Jesus;
Never shall we know the garden of agony.
He gives us a few drops from His chalice,
But reserves for Himself all the gall.

The language of Jesus is not the
Language of earthly bridegrooms.
His silence bespeaks the mysteries
He is amassing for His spouses.

To crown us better when He calls us to
The eternal banquet, the real nuptials,
Jesus does not think twice before
Sending us the graces of suffering.

After having tried us, He gives us joy.
One day we shall reap rejoicing!
The more we shall have suffered,
The more radiant this day will be.

So ravishing, so beautiful, so sweet…
This day which will have no setting!
Let us give without counting the cost.
Countless treasures will be given in exchange!

IN ANTICIPATION

[Adapted From the Letters of Marie to Thérèse]

The night of life will come
Just as the night of this day.
The morning of eternity will be
Without a night and a tomorrow.

Then, clothed in glory,
Measured by humiliations,
You shall bless the Cross.
Remember: all passes, except Love.

On earth, Jesus is not generous with His
Joys; these would harm celestial goods.
He who dreams of nothing but glory
Deprives in order to enrich.

If His little fiancée were to see His
Smile or hear the sound of His voice,
She would no longer live; she would
Die of love.

That is why He hides Himself.
That is why He is silent.
But after the dream of this life
He will speak to His little spouse forever.

You are privileged among all others.
He has gathered your tears in His heart.
They are mingled with His own, for you
Are one with your Spouse.

In heaven, there is great jubilation:
The angels weave crowns,
The cherubim gather flowers,
The enraptured saints ponder glory.

In His sweet voice, the Beloved boasts:
They are preparing for My wedding.
There is a little soul upon whom
I have cast a glance of love.

She has understood Me and has
Given herself to Me; I am happy
To have for Myself alone this heart
That ravishes Me with love.

Little fiancée, My retinue is approaching.
Rise my spouse from the earth of exile
And come unite yourself to me, for
I have chosen you from eternity.

SOJOURN
[Adapted From the Letters of Thérèse to Marie]

For the orpheline de Bérésina, there
Are no longer anything but heavenly
Joys filled with good resolutions.

Joys in which everything created,
Which is nothing, gives room for
The uncreated, which is reality.

Tomorrow, she will be the bride of
Jesus, the bride of Him whose face was
Hidden and whom no one recognized.

What an alliance, what a future: the
Day of everlasting memory, the day
Of eternal nuptials.

Her Fiancé is having her travel through
Fertile and magnificent countries, but,
Alas, night obscures all these marvels.

She is not saddened by this but is happy
To follow her Fiancé—so ravishing is her
Love for Him even when He is silent.

For us who understand His tears in this
Valley of exile, His resplendent Face will
Be shown to us in the fatherland.

This will be the ecstasy: the eternal union
Of glory with our Spouse, because He found
Us worthy to endure the crucible of suffering.

THEOLOGY 101
[Adapted From the Letters of Thérèse to Marie]

Without showing Himself, without making His voice heard,
Jesus teaches His disciples in secret the science of Love.
Since it is love alone that can make one pleasing to God,
This science is the only good one must ambition to learn.

Abandonment of the little child who sleeps without fear in
His Father's arms is the only road which leads to this
Divine furnace; it is confidence and nothing but confidence
That must lead to Love.

Jesus does not ask for great actions, He has no need of
Works but only of love; when He said, "Give me to drink,"
It was the love of His poor creatures that the Creator of
The universe was asking for—He was thirsty for love.

Jesus is parched more than ever; He meets with only the
Ungrateful and indifferent, even among His own disciples.
Few hearts give themselves to Him without any reservations,
Few hearts understand all the tenderness of His infinite Love.

To love Jesus, to be His victim of love, the weaker one is,
Without desires or virtues, the more suited one is for the
Workings of this consuming and transforming Love, for the
Lord chooses the little ones to confound the great ones.

The truly poor in spirit must look for Him from afar: in Lowliness, in nothingness; then, however far His little Children may have wandered, Jesus will find and transform Them in flames of Love.

PRICELESS
[Adapted From the Letters of Marie to Thérèse]

The little Thérèse has grown up, and still she is
Always the little one, always the Benjamin,
Always the darling whom Jesus holds by the hand.

As for herself, she still goes on, as in days gone
By, gazing on the stars of heaven and closing her
Eyes to all things here below.

Her heavenly spouse rocks her gently on His
Heart, smiles at her abandonment, gathers for
Her thousands of treasures.

So little Thérèse is disturbed about nothing but
Loving Jesus; she is His privileged spouse to whom
He confides His sweet secrets.

Just as the wicked are possessed by the devil, she
Is absolutely possessed by good Jesus, she is an
Echo from His Sacred Heart.

It is no wonder that Jesus is desirous of gathering
His golden cluster, His little flower, for she dreams
Only of looking above, of working for heaven.

So precious is the fortune little Thérèse possesses
That Jesus looks upon her desires, her nothings,
As extraordinary works of martyrdom.

Céline Martin

4

CÉLINE MARTIN
(1869–1959)

"Delicate but possessed of astonishing endurance,"[1] Céline, the seventh of the nine Martin children, was born on April 28, 1869. From her earliest years, she exhibited a keen religious sensibility. According to her mother, Zélie, "Little Céline is completely inclined to virtue; it is the innermost feeling of her person. She has a pure soul and loathes evil."[2] Far from being shy and reserved, however, Céline was considered courageous and forthright in her dealings with others, so much so that her father, Louis, dubbed her "The Intrepid."

Céline was not quite four when Thérèse was born. In the ensuing years, especially after the death of their mother in 1877, the two became inseparable, sharing a unique fusion of souls— first as childhood playmates, then as young adults, and finally as Carmelites. In the familial abode of Les Buissonnets (the Lisieux homestead), Céline and Thérèse shared their "struggles and sufferings."[3] They became "spiritual sisters" and "formed bonds…stronger than blood."[4]

Beyond adjusting to the loss of their mother, they eventually had to come to terms with the departure of their second oldest sister, Pauline, to Carmel. Thérèse was nothing short of inconsolable, feeling yet again the pangs of abandonment over the absence of her chosen pseudo-mother figure. "Céline felt this separation all the more keenly since it was followed not long after by Thérèse's illness,"[5] which, over a period of roughly five months, "ended with an apparition of the Blessed Virgin and a miraculous cure."[6] Céline further endured the anguish of watching Thérèse take leave of their oldest sister, Marie, also bound for Carmel. This event exacerbated Thérèse's hypersensitive temperament, giving rise to free-floating anxiety, often manifesting itself in the form of scruples. Despite this inner turmoil, Céline, as a firsthand witness, claimed that Thérèse never "let slip any opportunity to make sacrifices to God."[7]

Determined to take control of the emotional rollercoaster she had been riding, Thérèse, with the grace of God (and one might well imagine, the support and encouragement of Céline), "underwent on Christmas Eve 1886 her 'conversion'; it was a change that made her look extraordinarily self-possessed and courageous from then on. As she says herself: 'Jesus made me strong, and from that blessed night onwards I was never again overcome in battle…On the contrary, I began to 'rejoice like a champion to run my course.'"[8]

For some months thereafter, Céline and Thérèse experienced an idyllic existence, more or less, especially insofar as spiritual matters were concerned. "Their life on earth," according to Thérèse, "was the ideal of happiness."[9] The nature and scope of the intimate relationship they shared during this epoch was eloquently memorialized by Thérèse in her autobiography:

> How sweet were the conversations we held each evening in the belvedere! With enraptured gaze we beheld the white moon rising quietly behind the tall trees, the silvery rays it was casting upon sleeping nature, the bright stars twinkling in the deep skies, the light breath of the evening breeze making the snowy clouds float easily

along; all this raised our souls to heaven, that beautiful heaven whose "obverse side" alone we were able to contemplate…It appears we were receiving graces like those granted to the great saints…Doubt was impossible, faith and hope were unnecessary, and Love made us find on earth the One whom we were seeking.[10]

The sublimity of these mutual and reciprocal interludes was likewise echoed by Céline: "Our union became so intimate that I hesitate to try to picture it in words, fearing to mar its beauty…Each evening, our hands clasped in each other's, our glance contemplating the immensity of the heavens, we spoke of that Life that will never end…Where were we when, lost, so to speak, to ourselves, our voices would fade into silence? Where were we then?—I ask myself."[11]

To be sure, they served as unparalleled confidantes to each other. And it was in this context that Thérèse shared with Céline the utmost desire of her being: to become a Carmelite. Céline, of course, was elated. This was especially significant, given that Céline too sought the same goal, but without a moment's fuss or hesitation, "gave way to Thérèse, allowing her to enter the convent first…even though this might have endangered her own chances of entering the convent of her choice."[12] Not only did she temporarily suspend her own aspirations, but she wholeheartedly backed Thérèse in the many hardships she encountered prior to her admission to Carmel at the age of fifteen—most prominent among these: her face-to-face appeal to Pope Leo XIII. Accompanied by their father, Céline and Thérèse, along with members of the Bayeux-Lisieux diocese, embarked upon a "pilgrimage to Rome…to celebrate the golden jubilee of Leo XIII's ordination to the priesthood."[13]

Having found little success in acquiring the permission of the local ecclesiastical authorities to enter Carmel at fifteen, Thérèse was doggedly bound to plead her cause to the Supreme Pontiff himself. During the scheduled audience with Leo XIII, members of the entourage were forbidden to speak to the Pope as they were individually introduced. Although Thérèse had previously planned to speak—and even prepared what she would say—when the moment came, she felt her "courage weaken,"[14] whereupon she looked in the direction of her dear Céline who had but one word for her: "Speak!"[15] Which is precisely what she did. Much to her chagrin and disappointment, however, she was dismissed with his utterance: "Go...go. You will enter if God wills it."[16]

Back in Lisieux, despite the odds of success, Thérèse—and by extension, Céline—never ceased hoping against hope. And not without providential justification: because God "did not allow creatures to do what they willed but what He willed,"[17] Thérèse was granted permission to enter Carmel on April 9, 1888, three months after her fifteenth birthday. "'In kissing her goodbye at the door of the monastery,'Céline wrote, 'I had to lean trembling against the wall...yet I did not cry. I wanted with all my heart to give her to Jesus, and He, in return, clothed me with His strength.'"[18] Later, in experiencing the sting of Thérèse's absence, Céline acknowledged, "I feel emptiness everywhere," to which Thérèse responded, "Yes, life is painful for us...Let us raise ourselves above what is passing away...let us keep ourselves a distance from the earth...let us lay the axe to the root of the tree... Jesus is asking ALL, ALL, ALL."[19] Moreover, Thérèse genuinely believed in the permanency of their bond, claiming that, "if the Ocean separated us we would still stay united, for our desires are the same and our hearts beat together."[20]

A period of six years elapsed before Céline joined Thérèse and her sisters in Carmel. In the interim, Céline assumed the role of caretaker for her ailing father. Louis suffered a series of strokes, replete with paralysis; to add insult to injury, his mental faculties progressively deteriorated, causing memory lapses, aimless wandering, and hallucinations—the most notorious of which caused him to brandish a gun, fearing his household was under attack. He was forcibly disarmed and thereafter committed to Bon Sauveur, a hospital for the mentally ill, by his brother-in-law, Isidore Guérin. He remained there for three years under the watchful eye of Céline—the one on whom he could rely "to guide his last steps."[21] Though he was not cured, he was no longer a flight risk since his legs had become almost entirely paralyzed. His return to Lisieux was marked by occasional bouts of agitation and depression, but on the whole, he was calm and compliant. In June 1894 he suffered a heart attack, which signaled the beginning of the end for the seventy-year-old invalid. In mid-July he fell out of bed, and a short two weeks later, on July 29, "God broke the bonds of His incomparable servant and called him to his eternal reward."[22]

Apart from the grief that naturally accompanies the death of a beloved parent, the Martin sisters were primed to welcome Céline into their ranks. Thérèse in particular wanted to secure her safe arrival, for she worried that Céline would be sullied by the world's "social demands."[23] "Thérèse admits that after her Profession her single ardent desire was to have Céline in the Carmel as soon as possible. 'I desired this happiness not from natural impulse, but for her soul's sake, so that she too might travel along my little way.'"[24] As for Céline, God similarly broke the bonds "which held his dear fiancée in the world because she had accomplished her mission."[25] And thus, "freed of this obligation, she could at last satisfy her religious aspirations."[26] After disentangling her "muddled affairs,"[27] Céline (through the intercession of their father, in Thérèse's opinion) entered Carmel on September 14, 1894.

Oozing with sincerity and chomping at the bit to be a perfect nun, Céline (Sister Geneviève of the Holy Face) launched her monastic lifestyle with the zeal of a marathon runner sprinting to the finish line. The race, however, had scarcely begun. Her industrious efforts produced exhaustion, not valor. Her extreme asceticism was punitive, not salvific. Her grandiose intentions yielded depression, not virtue. Her perfectionism led to distraction, not humility. In short, she was in dire need of guidance. True to form, Thérèse hastened to her rescue. In her post as assistant novice mistress, she sought to align Céline's misdirected inclinations with a paradigm uniquely her own. "Thérèse had been slowly carving out another way, rooted not in grand deeds, asceticism and the image of God who exacts perfection, but in avoiding all self-seeking, in unseen acts of personal kindness within the grasp of an ordinary soul, and a God whom she could trust to love her despite her flaws."[28] In her autobiography, Thérèse unashamedly confessed, "It is impossible for me to grow up, and so I must bear with myself such as I am with all my imperfections. But I want to seek out a means of going to heaven by a little way, a way that is very straight, very short, and totally new."[29] She then conjured up the image of an elevator as the instrumental means to her consummatory end:

> I wanted to find an elevator which would raise me to Jesus, for I am too small to climb the rough stairway of perfection. I searched, then, in the Scriptures for some sign of this elevator, the object of my desires, and I

read these words coming from the mouth of Eternal Wisdom: 'Whoever is a LITTLE ONE, let him come to me.' And so I succeeded. I felt I had found what I was looking for…The elevator which must raise me to heaven is Your arms, O Jesus! And for this I had no need to grow up, but rather I had to remain little and become this more and more.[30]

This was precisely the lesson that Thérèse relentlessly desired to teach Céline.

Whether in her capacity as assistant novice mistress or simply as a member of her religious community, Thérèse's practical wisdom and spiritual prudence were a source of inspiration to all. According to Céline, "though not everybody admitted it, all went to her for guidance at one time or another; she was not soft or easy-going, but people turned to her out of a natural need for truth. Some of the older nuns went to her secretly, like Nicodemus, when they needed advice for themselves."[31] Céline herself openly yearned for Thérèse's counsel and direction and picked her brain whenever the opportunity arose. Not only did Céline candidly acknowledge her deficiencies, but she readily credited Thérèse for setting her straight:

Without seeking personal consolation, she tried to dissipate the illusions, the prejudices that I brought in from the world. In spite of a certain imperviousness God's grace supplies, all the same it is impossible not to be tainted. I was too long plunged into it not to have retained some of the false colors…She taught me the art of war, pointing out the dangers, the ways to conquer the enemy, the manner of using arms. She guided me step by step in the battles of each day…She made me find my joy in being a "very little soul" which God was obliged ceaselessly to uphold because I was no more than weakness and imperfection.[32]

These lessons, which captivated Céline and took root in her heart, made her a charter member of Thérèse's "Little Way" of self-surrender, her school of "Spiritual Childhood" whose raison d'être for those enrolled included (then and now): "joyous humility, complete confidence in Merciful Love, total abandonment to the divine will, exquisite art of giving pleasure to God in the least things of life, [and] a profound, living knowledge of the Fatherhood of God."[33]

Hardly had Céline and Thérèse spent three years together as Carmelites when the latter was in the slow burn of one of the era's most virulent and derelict diseases: tuberculosis (or "consumption," as it was then generally known). Thérèse's case was particularly insidious because, in addition to infiltrating her lungs, the disease also invaded her intestines, causing gangrene. Her suffering was incalculable, especially considering that the then Prioress of the Carmel, Mother Marie de Gonzague, refused to allow Thérèse to receive morphine, which could have substantially mitigated her agony. The Prioress did, however, appoint Céline as assistant infirmarian and authorized her to care for Thérèse. Which primarily amounted to providing her with emotional and spiritual comfort. As an eyewitness to Thérèse's protracted illness and eventual death, Céline later testified at the diocesan tribunal that "in the midst of all her sufferings the Servant of God preserved her serenity," that "her peace was unshakable," and that her words "always bore the stamp of perfect resignation."[34] As she lay dying,

> To Pauline, Thérèse affirmed that "everything is grace." And to Marie, she announced her famous "shower of roses." But it was for Céline that she reserved the best of her affection, knowing that it was she who would suffer the most from her death: "Ah…It is my little sister Geneviève who will feel my departure the most." She even called her right side "Thérèse's side" and her left side "Céline's side." They were two lifelong accomplices, two birds nesting forever in the arch of divine Love.[35]

With the death of Thérèse and the publication of *Histoire d'Une Ame* (*Story of a Soul*) a year later, a tsunami of interest was unleashed on the world. Irrespective of age or station in life, people everywhere clamored to know more about Thérèse—not the least of which included "what this 'saintly' nun looked like."[36] Numerous photographs had been taken of Thérèse by Céline who, upon her entrance to Carmel, was given permission to bring her camera. "However, to Céline the word saint evoked not photographs, but romantic religious art—luminous faces of celestial beauty."[37] Thus, "Céline began to retouch the photographs… Still dissatisfied, she decided to paint a portrait of Thérèse, a portrait less concerned with the details of her features than with radiating saintliness."[38] Over time, "Céline's portraits became more fanciful. She added roses, heavenly rays of light, and idealized Thérèse's features."[39] When Thérèse's actual photographs came to light, Céline was harshly criticized for attempting to dupe the public. According to author and Theresian scholar, Patricia

O'Connor, "It is unlikely that Céline intentionally distorted her sister. Undoubtedly her photographs failed to convey all that she saw in Thérèse. But Céline was also in the grip of a fixated idea. She thought art a higher expression of truth than photography, and she thought herself an artist."[40] As documented in her obituary "Circular," Céline "was not insensitive to the criticisms that were not infrequently leveled at her work. Evidently, her taste was appreciated in her own time...All the same she made use of a talent that was real."[41]

Céline spent the remainder of her long life enthusiastically promoting the doctrine of Thérèse's "Little Way of Spiritual Childhood." Her tireless efforts to arouse, sustain, and increase the cult of her beloved sister and soul mate were many and varied; her numerous paintings and publications only scratch the surface of her work in this regard. Whether in "classifying the archives" or maintaining "a vast correspondence," her responsibilities revolved around a singular purpose: "to be of service in some such way, for the glory of God and of my sister Thérèse."[42] Céline's old age was plagued by a plethora of infirmities, including acute rheumatism, sciatica, gout, uremia, congestive heart failure, and impaired hearing and vision, to name but a few. These maladies notwithstanding, "her whole energy was unleashed in the struggle to affirm in its entire scope Thérèse's message."[43] Even in her advanced years, Céline validated and espoused in word and deed the fundamental tenets of Thérèse's "last will and testament," namely, simplicity, humility, and confidence—as perhaps best exemplified when, at the age of eighty-eight, she somewhat facetiously reminisced:

> My long life ends by superimposed zeros. How true! I
> have given myself fatigue, labored, suffered much, but

what are these works themselves in an unworthy crea-
ture like myself—unprofitable earth! Happy shall I be
if my zeros are not too often stained with ink marks!
Still that corresponds completely with my wish to have
nothing but a page of zeros to offer God, for I prefer
that there be nothing in me to reward or to praise. I
want to be clothed with the works of Jesus, that accord-
ing to those works my Father in Heaven may judge and
love me.[44]

In the view of those who kept vigil at her bedside, "there
was something majestic about the dying nun, a supreme tran-
quility, wherein could be read the certitude of the welcome full
of tenderness that her Father would give her."[45] And thus it was
that Céline, "under the watch of a Community who venerated
in her life the last echo of a precious past,"[46] surrendered her
spirit on February 25, 1959 at the age of eighty-nine years and
ten months.

SISTERS TWICE OVER
[Adapted From the Letters of Thérèse to Céline]

The same soul animates us: our joys, our pains, our
Desires are the same, and our hearts beat together.
In union, we are still two; in unity, we are only one.

This is continuing in Carmel, for Jesus has already
Placed on your finger the ring of the espousals.
He wants to be the sole Master of your soul.

We are truly Sisters in the full strength of the term.
A day without suffering is a day lost for a Carmelite.
It is the same for you as a Carmelite at heart.

Jesus is begging this sorrow, this agony from us.
He needs it for souls and for our soul's recompense.
Like His beloved saints, His ambitions for us are great.

This is the only means of preparing us know Him as
He knows Himself and to become Gods ourselves.
Together let us lay the axe to the root of the tree.

Tears the wicked make Him shed are dried by our love.
Jesus does not look at the grandeur or the difficulty of
Actions as much as the love which goes to making them.

Since you have chosen Him and He has chosen you first,
Your soul is a lily immortelle; the tempest cannot make
The yellow of its stamen fall on its white scented calyx.

At this Lily's side, Jesus has placed its faithful companion.
Jesus asks ALL from His two lilies; He wills to leave them
Nothing but their white dress...Oh, what a destiny!

SEPARATION ANXIETY
[Adapted From the Letters of Céline to Thérèse]

What sadness, what heartaches for Céline.
Being separated from you, without any
Support, without any counsel, causes
Bitter tears at the feet of Jesus.

Everything is filled with memories of you:
Our long chats, resolutions, dreams of sanctity.
What conformity of ideas, of affections.
What sweet outpourings we used to have.

In this profound silence, witnessed only by
The stars and the moon, there were two
Souls—it seems to me they make up only
One—and what beautiful language was theirs!

In your absence, exile, emptiness everywhere.
But don't be disturbed by my complaints, for
When we cease to suffer, we cease to love.
The absence of the Cross is the absence of life.

Ah! it's true that all passes, but all is so long!
However, Jesus is here; He takes the place of all.
What a blessed moment when He will say to us:
Now it is my turn.

A MOMENT BETWEEN TWO ETERNITIES
[Adapted From the Letters of Thérèse to Céline]

Jesus has designs of an indescribable
Love for His little Lily-Immortelle.
The Martyrdom is beginning: to suffer
And to be despised.
What bitterness but what glory.
Each new agony of her heart is like a
Light breeze which will carry to Jesus
The perfume of His lily.

The love Jesus has for her demands ALL.
He does not want to set any limit to
His Lily's SANCTITY.
Infinity has no limits, no bottom, no shore.
Eternity is advancing in great strides.
Soon a more radiant Sun will light up its
Splendors: ethereal oceans, infinite horizons.
Immensity will be the deified domain!

Jesus has done foolish things for Céline;
Let Céline do foolish things for Jesus.
Love is repaid by love alone!
The wounds of love are healed only by love.
To those who love more, He gives more.
Be adorned by the Sun of His love; be the
Faithful shadow of Jesus.
There is only Jesus who is, all the rest is not.

Suffer in peace with all that Jesus wills.
Suffering united to His suffering is what
Delights His Heart the most.
How it costs to give Jesus what He asks,
Without joy, without courage, without strength!
Unknown martyrdom, without honor, without
Triumph, is love pushed to the point of heroism!
Get to work through love.

Attach yourself to Jesus alone by detaching
Yourself from His consolations.
Love Him unto folly by saving souls for Him.
Souls are being lost like flakes of snow!
Be tireless in braving the soldiers of this
World in order to reach Him.
Fly to the mountain of love where the beautiful
Lily of your soul is to be found.

CONTEMPLATING IMMENSITY
[Adapted From the Letters of Céline to Thérèse]

My dear confidante, you are the reality
While I am only your shadow.
The little Atom is united to the Grain
Of Sand in the Heart of Jesus.
We two cannot be separated.

Let us suffer, let us give our whole life,
All our blood, all the strength of our
Soul and our heart for Jesus!
The Cross that we are carrying
Is very bitter.

It isn't the big things that wound our
Heart the most, but little nothings.
The bird fears the bullet less than the
Hunter's rifle; this serves to detach us
From earth, looking upon it as transitory.

There is nothing that does not speak of exile.
Our heart is filled with melancholy but
Let us trust Jesus, for soon we shall rejoice
Over our sorrows—everything in them is
Visibly marked with His divine finger.

Our soul is the harp of Jesus; this harp alone
Knows for what concerts it is employed.
He touches the most sensitive chords.
Our mystical union with Jesus will engender
Souls for heaven.

A MARTIN ORIGINAL
[Adapted From the Letters of Thérèse to Céline]

The little Céline flower, unknown on earth,
Its white corolla filled with mystery, its
White calyx inwardly red, purpled with its
Own blood: a perfect image of your soul.

Without wilting it, the sun and rain
Fall upon this unknown flower.
Instead of retarding it, the rigors of
Winter make it grow and blossom.

Useless by profane eyes, fruitful and
Powerful in the eyes of Jesus.
A ray from His Heart can make
His flower bloom for eternity.

No one dreams of plucking it; Jesus
Alone has created it for Himself.
Like a vigilant bee, He gathers honey
Contained within its multiple calyxes.

While suffering her martyrdom, Jesus wills
That His little flower love Him to infinity.
This union will affect marvels: the children,
The souls of His virginal spouse.

A FAITHFUL ECHO
[Adapted From the Letters of Thérèse to Céline]

Let us make our heart a garden of
Delights where Jesus may come to rest.
Let us plant only lilies, since other
Flowers can be cultivated by other souls.
Virgins alone can give lilies to Jesus.

To be virgin we must think only of the
Spouse who allows nothing around Him
That is not virgin: He is the Virgin of virgins.
Born by His will of a Lily, He loves to find
Himself in virgin hearts.

Ah, Céline, how blessed we are for having
Been chosen by the Spouse of Virgins!
Thérèse can do nothing without Céline.
The two are needed to complete a work.
Céline must finish what Thérèse has begun.

This foreign land has for us only wild plants
And thorns: the portion given to our divine
Spouse in the exile of life.
The day of salvation dawns when the tears
Of Jesus are the smile of a soul.

The image of this world is passing, the shadows
Are lengthening; our native land approaches.
From our dear Father's radiant head we shall
See His white hairs coming forth, each one will
Be like a sun that will give us joy and happiness.

When looking at us Jesus will say: how beautiful
Is the chase generation of virgin souls!
Let us always remain the lilies of Jesus!
From our two hearts let us make one.
What a mystery is our grandeur in Jesus!

SPIRITUAL TWINSHIP
[Adapted From the Letters of Thérèse to Céline]

Jesus has many daisies in His meadow.
They each receive the rays of the Sun.
Jesus is the divine Sun; the daisies are
His spouses, the virgins.

One day, the Spouse of virgins bent down
To earth and united tightly two little buds.
Scarcely open, their stems were merged
Into a single one.

These little flowers, Céline and Thérèse,
Now a double daisy, blossomed; and
Fixing its eyes on the Divine Sun,
Accomplishes its mission which is one.

Jesus joined our hearts in so marvelous
A way that what makes one heart beat
Makes the other heart throb: our hearts
Make only one in Him.

Without Him, no discourse has any charms.
He raised us, attracted us together, a
Unity of souls and minds, above the fragile
Things of this world.

In the retreat of the heart, He instructs us.
Our mission is sublime: form evangelical
Workers who will save thousands of souls
And fill the empty places in heaven!

STALLED

[Adapted From the Letters of Céline to Thérèse]

The many lights, the miracles of graces,
The strange mysteries taking place
In the soul of my Thérèse!
Our Lord is so good to you!

You speak to your little Céline about
Beautiful nature presented to my gaze,
About infinite horizons unfolding before me.
This does me good!

But, alas, the eye becomes accustomed to
Everything, even to the most beautiful things.
The attraction of all that is not our Divine Charm
Pales and wears out.

Unless He gives life to objects by His glance
And His presence, we do not find Him.
I have lost the power to distinguish between
The beautiful and the ugly.

I question immensity; I try to dream but cannot.
Nothing gives me any response.
I am like a donkey grazing on the highway
Without knowing what it is doing!

My state is to see without seeing, to
Understand without understanding.
Supported without any support, I go on.
My spirit is flattened without highs or lows.

All has been covered by the same veneer.
One mysterious void envelops my mind.
I am reduced to the state of the log being
Consumed under the ashes.

I am in darkness, in total incapacity, thinking
Of nothing: not Jesus, not souls.
Unable to stop at anything tangible,
My soul is downcast.

MIDDAY

[Adapted From the Letters of Céline to Thérèse]

The morning of life is past; now it is noon, so
Heavy, so crushing, so dry, so sad...
At present, I am like a piece of wood; there is
No longer anything to draw on from within me.
There is always nothing, always the dark night.
My soul is plunged into unfathomable depths.

Incapable of doing good, I can only desire good.
My aridity is such that I no longer see clearly
Through the fog of my continual malaise.
To reign over me, God will have to break my
Inner certitude; my tortured heart needs the
Bare cross and the most bitter tribulation.

Suffering from scruples, I can no longer breathe.
Nothing pleases me, except to be the drop of dew
Refreshing the calyx of the Flower of the fields.
A single drop of dew is more than sufficient for
Jesus: it is an ocean for Him that both consoles
And quenches His thirst.

In this I find comfort, along with the conviction that
I am already a daughter of Saint John of the Cross
And Saint Teresa since my lot is to suffer and be
Despised; God is thus not asking me to practice many
Virtues, to produce aspirations divinely scented, but
To believe that love alone suffices.

NOT AS THE WORLD GIVES
[Adapted From the Letters of Thérèse to Céline]

How easy it is to please Jesus, to delight His Heart.
One has only to love Him, without looking at one's
Self, without examining one's faults too much,
Drawing profit from everything—the good and the
Bad alike.

When Jesus wills to take for Himself the sweetness
Of giving, it would not be very gracious to refuse.
Allow Him to take and give all He wills, for perfection
Consists in doing His will; in peace, in abandonment,
Do all through love.

Never get discouraged; seek opportunities, nothings,
Which please Jesus more than the mastery of the
World or even martyrdom suffered with generosity.
The smallest thing—a smile, a friendly word—is
Precious in His divine eyes.

Jesus is a hidden treasure, an inestimable good which
Few souls can find, for the world loves what sparkles,
And leads souls to springs without water; nevertheless,
It is obliged to smell the perfumes that are exhaled to
Purify the empoisoned air it never ceases to breathe in.

But it is from within that the King of kings shines with
All His glory; what joy to pass as fools in the eyes of
The world and to suffer for Him who loves unto folly.
To be like Jesus, one must hide oneself, be unknown,
Accounted for nothing, and possess childlike docility.

Let the little exile be sad without being sad, having no
Other duty but to love; fear nothing and take heart
Since a great serenity will follow the rampant storm.
Soon, Jesus will stand up to save all the meek and
Humble of the earth.

JESUS' PREDILECTION
[Adapted From the Letters of Thérèse to Céline]

Like a pure drop of dew, simplicity is the
Distinctive characteristic of Céline's heart.
Céline is a little drop of dew hidden in the
Divine corolla of the beautiful Lily of the
Valleys, the dew that has descended from
Heaven, its homeland.

During the night of life, its mission is to hide
Itself in the heart of the Flower of the fields.
No human eye is to discover it there, only the
Calyx possessing the little drop will know its
Freshness; to be His, the blessed Céline-flower
Of Jesus must aspire to remain little in this way.

When the Flower of the fields becomes the
Sun of Justice, He will cast on the poor drop
Of dew one of His rays of love, making it
Sparkle like a precious diamond which will
Have become like Him, thus astonishing those
Who considered the drop of dew as useless.

Then, the divine Star, gazing at His drop of dew,
Will draw it to Himself; it will ascend like a light
Vapor and go to place itself for eternity in the
Bosom of the burning furnace of uncreated love.
There it will be forever united to Him, fulfilling
The purpose for which it was created.

Just as on earth it had been the faithful companion
Of His exile, His insults, in the same way it will
Reign forever in heaven, remaining always Jesus'
Drop of dew; what a privilege to be called to so
Holy and lofty a mission, climaxing in an eternal
Face to Face.

RESCUED AT SEA

[Adapted From the Letters of Thérèse to Céline]

In the midst of stormy waves, Céline is all alone
In a little boat; the land has disappeared from
Her eyes, she does not know where she is going,
Whether she is advancing or going backward,
Close or far from port.

The more the shore recedes, the vaster the ocean
Appears; her knowledge is reduced to nothing.
Since she does not know how to control the rudder,
She has to abandon herself and allow her sail to
Flutter in the wind.

But Jesus is there, sleeping peacefully as in days
Gone by, in the boat of the fishermen of Galilee.
Céline neither sees Him nor hears His voice, for
Night has fallen and the wind is blowing; she sees
Only the darkness as Jesus continues to sleep.

If He were to awaken for but an instant, He would
Have only to command the wind and sea to restore
Calm, and the night would become brighter than day.
Céline would see the divine glance of Jesus, and her
Soul would be consoled.

In His dear spouse's boat, Our Lord finds the pillow
Of Céline's heart; there He is at home and happy.
But how can He be happy while His spouse suffers,
While she vigilantly keeps watch, while His divine
Face remains hidden from her?

Céline must recall that her Beloved is also a bundle
Of myrrh, of suffering; and it is in this way that
Jesus rests on Céline's heavy and tear-filled heart.
The wind of sorrow that pushes her boat is the wind
Of love which is swifter than lightning.

Soon the dawn will come and Jesus will say to Céline:
"You have given me the only home that every heart
Is unwilling to renounce, that is, yourself, and now I
Am giving you as a dwelling my eternal substance,
That is, Myself."

THE MARRIAGE CONTRACT
[Adapted From the Letters of Thérèse to Céline]

I, JESUS, ETERNAL WORD, THE ONLY SON OF GOD
AND OF THE VIRGIN MARY, espouse today Céline,
Henceforth GENEVIÈVE OF SAINT TERESA, exiled
Princess, poor and without titles, under the name of
KNIGHT OF LOVE OF SUFFERING AND CONTEMPT.

I am placing on her head the helmet of salvation
And grace so that her face may be hidden like Mine.
She will be the shepherdess of the one Lamb, who is
Becoming her Bridegroom; our union will bring forth
Souls more numerous than stars in the firmament.

I, the Flower of the Fields, the Lily of the Valleys,
Will give My Beloved for her nourishment the Wheat
Of the Elect, the Wine that brings forth Virgins.
She will receive this food from the humble and
Glorious Virgin Mary, the Mother of us both.

TOMORROW, THE DAY OF ETERNITY, I shall lift My
Helmet; My Beloved will see the brightness of My
Adorable Face, and she will receive for her Great
Reward the two other Persons of the BLESSED
TRINITY come to take possession of her soul.

After having shared the same hidden life, we shall
Enjoy in our kingdom the same GLORIES, the same
THRONE, the same PALM, and the same CROWN;
Our two hearts, united for eternity, will love with the
Same ETERNAL LOVE!!!...

CROSSING THE FINISH LINE
[Adapted From the Letters of Thérèse to Céline]

Do no fear, the poorer you are, the more Jesus will
Love you; He prefers to see you hitting against stones
In the night than walking in broad daylight on a path
Bedecked with flowers that could retard your progress.
He will go far, very far, in search of you if at times you
Wander off a little.

Line up humbly among the imperfect, esteem yourself
As a little soul whom God must sustain at each moment.
Never seek nor speak what appears great according to
The world; rather, tell Jesus that His name is like oil
Poured out, and that it is in this divine perfume you want
To bathe yourself entirely, far from the eyes of creatures.

All the works that occupy men—painting, sculpture, the arts—
Are subject to envy, creating vanity and affliction of spirit.
The only thing that is not envied is the last place; run to
The last place, no one will come to dispute you over it.
For real sanctity consists in humbling yourself, in bearing
Patiently with your imperfections.

You have learned well not to depend on your own strength
But on the strength of Him who, on the Cross, has overcome
The powers of hell; because you are convinced of your own
Nothingness, Good Jesus is more proud of your littleness and
Poverty than He is of having created millions of suns and the
Expanse of the Heavens!

Léonie Martin

5

LÉONIE MARTIN
(1863–1941)

Moody. Difficult. Backward. Capricious. Unmanageable. Inattentive. Unruly. Insubordinate. Volatile. Impulsive. Secretive. Troubled. Bizarre. Unpredictable. These are among the many words used to describe the ever-problematic "poor Léonie," the third daughter of Louis and Zélie Martin. In addition to these character flaws, which punctuated her childhood, adolescence, and young adulthood, Léonie was stricken with severe eczema, migraine headaches, and inexplicable convulsions. When compared with her sisters, she "did not have Marie's good sense, or Pauline's piety, or Céline's virtue, or Thérèse's intelligence…She was the black sheep of the Martin clan and stayed in the bacground."[1] Not so surprisingly, then, Léonie "always suffered from a sense of her inferiority."[2] Psychologically, this would perhaps explain in part her rebellious nature, which occasionally drifted into reaction formation. According to Zélie, "In a spirit of contradiction she would do precisely the contrary of what I wished, even when she would have wished to do the thing asked of her."[3] Yet, Zélie also recognized the inherent goodness of her daughter: "She is less favored…as regards to natural endowments, but, nevertheless, she has a heart that yearns to love and be loved."[4] Over time, this sentiment came to characterize the dominant demeanor of Léonie's life.

On the road to maturity, however, instability reigned, as blatantly illustrated through her four attempts to enter religious life. On a whim, and without securing the family's approval, Léonie decided to join the Poor Clares in Alençon, but given the austerity of their lifestyle, she lasted only two months. A short eight months later, she tried again, this time with the Visitation nuns at Caen; her stay with them ended after only six months. Some five years later, she yet again entered this same convent, remaining for a period of two years. Sadly, the third time was not the charm for Léonie. By this point in time—the year was 1895—Thérèse had already been a Carmelite for seven years and was both monitoring from afar and praying for the success of Léonie's vocation. Far from surrendering hope at this latest setback, Thérèse prophetically proclaimed to her sister Marie, "After my death I will make her return to the Visitation nuns, and she will persevere."[5] Which is precisely what happened. "Léonie was received back into the convent at Caen on January 29, 1899, and made her profession as Sister Françoise-Thérèse on July 2, 1900. She was to live there for almost forty-one years."[6]

Reading Thérèse's autobiography had a deep and abiding impact on the life and spiritual development of Léonie. It was in many respects the incentive for her own conversion: upon at last returning to the Visitation Monastery, "she decided from then on to follow in her Sainted sister's wake and dwell upon and study every day the profound secrets of spiritual childhood."[7] As recorded in her obituary "Circular," Léonie spoke of her canonized sister as her "beloved spiritual director," from whom "she derived the grace to accept her own deficiencies with joy."[8] And, in keeping with—and thus being a true devotee and disciple of—Thérèse's "Little Way," she wrote "that becoming little to the point of demolition was most sweet, since it was the shortest and surest way to reside in the Heart of Jesus."[9]

Like her beloved sister, Thérèse, and her devoted parents, Louis and Zélie, Léonie herself is well on the way to sainthood. The solemn opening of her official "Cause" took place in July of 2015. She now holds the title "Servant of God." As the "Process" moves forward, her Congregation harbors not a shred of doubt concerning her sanctity: "To this day, the Visitation nuns at Caen do indeed regard Léonie, the 'poor Léonie,' the 'darling Léonie,' as a saint."[10]

JESUS-VICTIM, YOUR SPOUSE AND MINE

[Adapted From the Letters of Thérèse to Léonie]

My dear little Visitandine, the thought of death
Is sweet; the brevity of life gives us courage.
It helps us bear the weariness of the road.
The light tribulations of this life prepare us
For an eternal weight of glory.

We are voyagers sailing toward the eternal shore.
We must merit the homeland of heaven.
We must suffer, we must fight!
The only happiness on earth is finding delightful
The lot Jesus is giving us.

Let us not refuse Him the least sacrifice.
To pick up a pin out of love can convert a soul.
It is Jesus alone who can give such value to our actions.
Let us love Him with all our strength, this God
Who becomes the beggar of our love!

Dear little Sister, I know that humility is your
Preferred virtue: to be unknown, counted as nothing.
Jesus is very much pleased with you!
He has placed His seal on your forehead.
Never will you receive any other lover but Him.

You will come off victorious from your trials,
And you will one day become a great saint!
Sacrifices do not fail to accompany the blessed home
In which your heart forever fixed its abode.
Without them, would the religious life be meritorious?

Do not forget to pray for the poorest of your sisters.
Ask Jesus that she be very faithful, that she be
Like you: happy to be the littlest, the last.
I love you with the Heart of our Celestial Spouse.
In Him we are living the same life for all eternity!

TRUE DEVOTEE
[Adapted From the Letters of Léonie to Thérèse]

How necessary it is that I, the prodigal child,
The little dove of the Ark, be helped from going
After the pleasures and vanities of the world.
It will take a lot to make me a saint.

What folly to be too attached to creatures.
The agonies to which foolish affections give rise:
Piety and pure love for Jesus impaired, perfection
Held back, scruples drawn in upon myself.

Pray for me, that I become a holy Visitandine.
Absolutely nothing is impossible with God!
Calvary gives me courage to suffer all that
Is most bitter.

In spite of thorns, God has given me great graces.
Envy my happiness; this is permitted.
It is the only thing worthy of envy on earth.
All the rest is but nothing.

Union with Jesus: the greatest desire of my soul.
For the one who possesses Jesus, possesses all!
Because our heart is made solely for God, He
Alone can fill it entirely; it is too big for the world.

You are ready to go see and lose yourself in God.
Surely you will be well received.
But I, alas, would arrive with empty hands.
And yet I have the boldness not to be afraid.

We have nothing to offer Jesus except faded flowers.
How many times have I not offered Him some!
Because I am so weak, I am depending on you.
Your knowledge always stops the runaway horse!

We are united in the Heart of Jesus, loved with
A tenderness which will last the blessed eternity.
May the divine Jesus always be the most precious
Token of your love.

Marie Guérin

6

MARIE GUÉRIN
(1870–1905)

Marie Guérin was the daughter of Isidore and Céline Guérin and the cousin and childhood playmate of Thérèse. She had an older sister, Jeanne, and a brother, Paul, who was stillborn. Accident prone as a youngster, she was described by her father as "a little imp, a quicksilver."[1] She played the piano and was said to have "a voice like a nightingale."[2] Her exceptional intelligence paled only in comparison to her scrupulosity, which we are told, persisted in varying degrees throughout the course of her life. Whereas Thérèse wanted to spend her Heaven doing good on earth, generically speaking, Marie had a more singular focus in mind: "As for me, when I am with the good God I will take care of exclusively scrupulous souls. This will be my specialty; I will spend my Heaven consoling them."[3]

Despite her "uneasy conscience" and bouts of "indecision,"[4] Marie at last decided to enter the Lisieux Carmel, already home to her four Martin cousins. During her novitiate—and informally well before—Marie (Sister Marie of the Eucharist) had the benefit and counsel of Thérèse's spiritual guidance as acting novice mistress. Recognizing Marie's proclivities toward "self-preoccupation" and "introspection," Thérèse "tried hard to reorient a heart too sensitive, to correct wayward behavior, to infuse selflessness, zeal for souls, humility in little conflicts of common life."[5] Without necessarily saying that she succeeded,

Thérèse herself acknowledged that "she possesses all the desirable qualities to become a saint."[6] Not too shabby an assessment from "the greatest saint of modern times," the title bestowed on Thérèse by Pope Pius X in 1914, well before her actual canonization. Marie Guérin died on April 14, 1905, after a protracted battle with tuberculosis. She was only thirty-five.

JUXTAPOSITION
[Adapted From the Letters of Marie Guérin to Thérèse]

Not made for healing the scrupulous,
Paris is a veritable hell.
I look upon it with horror.

Not knowing where to turn my eyes,
I flee from one nudity to meet another.
Out of curiosity I see evil everywhere.

Pursued by subjects of torment,
Every moment is a struggle.
I am not advancing in virtue.

Trials are beginning; I don't see
The future with a happy outlook.
This is a moment of great loathing.

My lot is interior suffering.
Experiencing a deadly ennui, I
Haven't the will power for anything.

God is pleased to break my heart.
When He wills to make me suffer,
It is always to my heart that He turns.

Allowing myself to live as worldly
People live, God has been forgotten.
My heart is empty and filled with sadness.

But I feel the most joy in Church; there
I can rest my eyes on the Tabernacle.
Never have I felt so much love for Communion.

Teach your little sister to walk with courage.
You have much fervor in God's service.
I am hardly born into the spiritual life.

Recommend my vocation to God.
If God wills to catch me in His nets,
I would throw myself into them with love.

I learned to make my first steps at Carmel.
Will it be there that I'll make my last?
How I'd like it to be so!

LOVE ALWAYS WINS
[Adapted From the Letters of Thérèse to Marie Guérin]

Don't listen to the devil; mock him.
You haven't committed the shadow of any evil.
Despise and pay no attention to temptations.

The evil one knows that he can't make a soul
That wants to belong to Jesus commit a sin,
So he tries to make the soul believe it has.

He wants to deprive Jesus of a loved Tabernacle.
Not being able to enter the sanctuary, He wants
It to remain empty, without any Master!

Jesus is there in the Tabernacle expressly for you.
He is burning with desire to enter your heart.
Without any fear, receive Jesus in peace and love!

It is impossible that a heart which rests
At the sight of the Tabernacle offend Jesus
To the point of not being able to receive Him.

Your heart is made to love Jesus passionately.
Pray that the beautiful years of your life
May not pass by in chimerical fears.

If you want to be healed, there is only one
Remedy: receive Communion often, very often.
Jesus hasn't placed this attraction in your soul for nothing.

Thank Jesus for having given you such a precious gift.
Your soul is so well made for consoling Him.
Love Him to folly for all those who don't.

You must not forget that Jesus is ALL.
Lose your little nothingness in His infinite ALL.
And think only of this uniquely lovable ALL.

May Jesus teach you the science of rejoicing
In infirmities; this is indeed a great grace.
Peace and quiet of heart are to be found only there.

Love is the only sure means of reaching perfection.
Jesus alone can understand the profundity of this word.
He knows how to return infinitely more than we can give Him.

Jesus is stricken by the sickness of love
Which is healed only through love.
He is thirsty for it, He is hungry for it!

The heart of His fiancée is what Jesus longs for.
Since you are already imprisoned in His nets,
Make Him loved by souls: this is your mission!

Céline Guérin

7

Céline Guérin
(1847–1900)

Upon the death of her sister-in-law, Zélie Martin, Céline Guérin and her husband, Isidore, assisted in raising to maturity their five nieces. To geographically—and emotionally—facilitate their newfound roles, they all but insisted that the Martins move from Alençon to Lisieux. Isidore searched high and low to find a suitable home to accommodate the family's needs. He was more than successful in this regard, locating a property "in a quiet section next to a park,"[1] henceforth called Les Buissonnets by the girls. Thérèse spoke of her time spent there as "that beautiful cradle of my childhood"[2] where "my life was truly happy."[3]

To say that Aunt Guérin was an affectionate, if doting, mother figure in the life of Thérèse would surely be a gross understatement. She was not overly indulgent, however, in dwelling on the often gut-wrenching and precarious circumstances underlying Thérèse's many trials and tribulations, especially insofar as her entrance to Carmel was concerned. Rather, she took a more measured and providential approach with Thérèse, always assuring her that "I see in all this the hand of God."[4] Thérèse, naturally, was observant of and grateful for the familial support with which she was showered: "Aunt...took care of me with a truly maternal solicitude."[5] In assuaging Thérèse's grief with prudent reasoning, she was instrumental in helping her confront reality on its own terms and thus embrace a level of maturity that characterized her disciplined life as a vowed religious.

More often than not—and given enough time—the parent's role is transposed with the child's. Such was the case between Aunt Guérin, acting in Zélie's stead, and Thérèse. Seven years into her vocation as a cloistered nun, Thérèse, now a mature young woman, received this impassioned request from her beloved Aunt: "I see myself filled with faults, my self love causes me much trouble in everything, it tortures me. You, you know so well how to pray to little Jesus, ask Him to cure me of this malady. I would need the gaiety of the Carmelite, and to attain it I do not know how to conduct myself. I count on you, little Thérèse, to obtain this grace for me."[6] The adage "What goes around comes around" strikes a familiar chord in what was apparently a mutually beneficial relationship.

Two weeks after Thérèse received this letter, Céline's daughter, Marie Guérin (Sister Marie of the Eucharist), would enter Carmel and, as fate would have it, find herself under the capable direction of her cousin Thérèse in her position as novice mistress. Interestingly, both mother and daughter were (whether by nature or nurture or a combination thereof) aided by Thérèse in combating the ebb and flow of scruples with which they struggled.

RSVP

[Adapted From the Letters of Céline Guérin to Thérèse]

Far from having the perfection you imagine
I am filled with faults; self-love in particular
Tortures me in this sad life of exile.

You know so well how to pray to little Jesus,
Ask Him to cure me of this malady; to obtain
This grace I need the gaiety of the Carmelite.

To you, my dear little Benjamin, I am turning:
Teach me, but not with just a look, how to go
About it, how to become a saint.

In all this I must see, be sure of, and very
Trusting in the hand of God's Providence,
Allowing myself to be directed entirely by Him.

Because sadness is too human a feeling which
Gives God grief, it must be chased away.
Cannot God change hearts in one instant?

Since God's good pleasure always comes before
Ours, I must learn to love all He wills as the only
Sure route to happiness and consolation.

Distance cannot diminish your kind affection; God
Himself formed this affection, uniting us and
Making up our joy here on earth.

MATERNAL SURROGATE

[Adapted From the Letters of Thérèse to Céline Guérin]

While growing up, your little daughter's heart
Was growing also in tenderness for you; it
Understands all it owes you and is begging Jesus
To bestow on you all the favors a child can
Dream for its dear mother.

To pay her debt, she entrusts her divine Spouse
With pouring out in profusion on dear Aunt the
Treasures of His love, thus returning to her all
The motherly acts of kindness with which her
Benjamin was surrounded during childhood.

Jesus comes to rest with delight in your home.
Just as He did at Bethany, the Beggar of love is
Always asking more in proportion to the gifts He
Receives; He honors the souls of His faithful by
Not giving much but asking much.

Since she has been on the mountain of Carmel,
Your little Thérèse feels more deeply the
Affection she has for you; the more she learns
To love Jesus, the greater becomes her fondness
For you.

Pray that your little daughter not abuse the grace
God is showering on her in the fertile valley of
Carmel; though imperfect and poor, may she grow
In wisdom as the divine Child Jesus grew and obtain
What she desires on the strength of her importunity.

Oh! Aunt, because of your virtues, your adopted child
Shall have a beautiful place at the heavenly banquet.
Her heart melts with gratitude for the overflowing
Measure of maternal love God poured into the depths
Of your soul.

When the saints and the angels learn that Sister
Thérèse of the Child Jesus has the honor of being your
Little daughter, they will not place her far from you in
The heavenly homeland; only there shall be expressed
What in human words is impossible.

Isidore Guérin

8

ISIDORE GUÉRIN
(1841–1909)

Isidore Guérin, a prominent pharmacist in the town of Lisieux, was the brother of Zélie, the Martin matriarch. After her death in 1877, when Thérèse's was just four and a half years old, he and his wife, Céline, persuaded Louis Martin—then in his mid-fifties and distraught over the loss of his beloved wife—to sell his business in Alençon and reestablish himself and his five daughters in Lisieux. There, the Guérins would be better equipped to assist with the girls' upbringing. This was especially important to Isidore, since he had been appointed deputy guardian of his nieces upon the death of their mother. Within a few months, the Martins settled into their new home, Les Buissonnets, on the outskirts of town.

In time, two of Thérèse's siblings, Pauline and, thereafter, Marie, decided to enter the Carmelite monastery situated in the town's center. Later, when Thérèse discerned that she too had a vocation to this contemplative lifestyle, she was, shockingly, only a young teenager. Having successfully procured her father's permission to enter Carmel at fifteen, Thérèse sought next to secure her Uncle Isidore's approval. This was a hard sell to say the least. She knew it would be. Dating back to her early childhood, Thérèse held some reservations about her uncle's temperament. In her autobiography, she recalls this impressionable episode: "I was very much frightened when he placed me on his knee and sang Blue Beard in a formidable tone of voice."[1] When she approached him on the matter of her entrance to Carmel, Uncle Guérin "uncompromisingly…countered Thérèse's tears with prudent reasoning: she was far too young."[2] Moreover, in his opinion, she was "a coddled child, an indulged child, oversensitive and under educated."[3] He, therefore, insisted that she not further entertain this prospect until she was at least seventeen.

While Thérèse saw this setback as "a sacrifice to offer Jesus,"[4] she was nevertheless sorely disappointed. But after a silence of nearly two weeks, she became increasingly more unsettled and anxious and thus enlisted the consolation and counsel of Pauline (Sister Agnes of Jesus). This face-to-face encounter at the Carmel so alarmed Pauline that she, at Thérèse's request, immediately wrote to Uncle Guérin to describe the dire circumstances of Thérèse's frenzied state. This letter read in part, "I come to you as to a Father, a real Father, not to plead but to explain the cause of this dear child…I think nothing, I want nothing, I understand nothing…Let God do what He will do!"[5] Pauline's compelling defense worked: upon reading the content of this appeal, Uncle Guérin rescinded his opposition to Thérèse's entrance. In the years that followed, he time and again endorsed the veracity of her vocation. After her death, he used his business savvy and connections, as well as his own financial resources, to expedite the publication of her autobiography.

HITHER AND YON
[Adapted From the Letters of Isidore Guérin to Thérèse]

Having no idea of the splendor and beauty of the
Heavens, the world longs for the mud in which it
Moves about: the infamies of corruption; the sound
Of malediction; the frightful and hideous wounds
Gnawing away at humanity; the distractions of Eden
On all sides; the Casino; the theatre; the dance; the
Concert; stores with articles of dress, jewelry, and art,
Attracting and arousing the covetousness of the passersby;
Splendid avenues; banks of rare flowers; shaded groves;
Crowds passing each other in rich carriages; the most
Attractive apparel; beautiful women soliciting the gaze of
Spectators, their eyes sparkling with unsatisfied pleasure...
From this crowd, drunk with desire, there is not a single
Cry, not a single aspiration coming from their heart to the
God who made the creature beautiful and who endowed
The genius to bring forth marvels of art and civilization.
The diaphanous robes of the guardian angels are flying far
Away, and Satan, baton in hand, beating time for the
Infernal dances.

But, behold, over there a modest building, surmounted
By the Cross, with neither gilding nor sculpture.
Wafting from within, the sound of gentle whispering
And the smell of fragrant incense.
Its inhabitants, dressed in brown robes, coarse woolens,
And hair shirts, nourish themselves on unrefined foods
And sleep on beds as hard as planks.

Their youth, their fortune, allowed them to shine in the
World and to enjoy the pleasures of life, but they
Preferred mortification and suffering.
With a chaste and pure love of a perfect and divine Being,
They satisfy their thirst for pleasure; His grace enkindles
In them a love that others cannot even suspect.
Consumed by the fires of this divine love, they offer up
Everything through prayer and self-sacrifice to be more
Conformed to their Master.
This cortege of Virgins, interceding and making reparation
For the feverish, dancing crowd, can be heard crying out to
Heaven: "Grace, Lord! Mercy and pardon!"

SWAN SONG
[Adapted From the Letters of Isidore Guérin to Thérèse]

I cannot hide it, I cannot analyze it: the pride of having
Such an adopted daughter; admiration for so great a
Courage and love of God; sadness against which human
Nature is defenseless when faced with a separation that
Appears eternal to it.
Faith and reason protest, but they cannot stop the painful
Groanings of the body when seeing itself deprived of one
Of its most precious members: you were your good
Mother's little pearl; your aged father's little queen; and
You are the most beautiful little flower of the lily-wreath
Crowning, giving a foretaste of the perfections of heaven.
The remembrance of your virtues and your innocence
Will never leave me.
Real family joys and love of one's own will receive their
Complete development and indestructibility only when
They are intermingled with the divine love that will
Consume them in the same ardor.

Never have I disputed the love of your Bridegroom, who
Is calling you.
Would one seek to hold back in the mire a dear one who
Extends her arms to the Savior after whom she has
Sighed for so long a time?
This would be a poorly understood affection, a selfishness.
Abandoned on your bed of pain, your image haunts me at
Each moment of the day.

Though I do not have a great love for life, I have not
Reached my little Thérèse's perfection, who would be
Happy at the coming of the Thief.
From the heights of heaven teach me to feel the flame
Of divine love which is consuming you and to which you
Desire to be united more intimately.
You will soon be one with the brilliance of the burning
Bush you have been fascinated by since childhood.
Until the eternal abode, A Dieu, my beloved child.

FAMILIAL GRATITUDE
[Adapted From the Letters of Thérèse to Céline and Isidore Guérin]

Little Thérèse sends to her dear relatives all the
Fruits of the Holy Spirit, particularly that of Joy!
She is begging God to reward them a hundredfold
For their touching kindness.

Her heart has aspirations for them that words are
Powerless to express; these, God alone can divine.
To Him she wants to entrust the wishes her heart
Is making for those who are so dear.

It seems only yesterday that good Uncle used to
Bounce her on his knees, singing the romance of
Bluebeard, with eyes that almost made her die of
Fright.

The weight of years has not taken away your OLD
Niece's memory; on the contrary, she is at an age
When memories of childhood have a particular
Charm.

She would like to reserve only consolations for her
Dear Uncle and Aunt; but, alas, God, who knows the
Rewards He is reserving for His friends, often loves to
Have them win His treasures by means of sacrifices.

Even in the midst of the trials He sends, God is filled
With tenderness and joy which will be greater still
When little Thérèse departs earth's exile for heaven.
God will then allow her to pour out His favors lavishly.

Good Jesus must have heard and understood perfectly
What she expects from Him: sweet martyrdom of love.
She is as cheerful as a finch because God is showing
Her that the only joy on earth is to accomplish His Will.

She shall speak to her dear relatives only in heaven
About her affection; for as long as she shall drag on
Here below, her pencil will not be able to adequately
Convey it…look only at your child's heart!

Marie de Gonzague

9

MARIE DE GONZAGUE
(1834–1904)

Known for her formidable temperament, Mother Marie de Gonzague spent twenty-one of her forty-four years in the Lisieux Carmel as Prioress. By most accounts, "her character was full of intense contradictions…Childlike, overflowing gaiety alternated abruptly with blackest melancholia; tenderest consideration for others with intolerable, haughty rudeness."[1] Thérèse was far less judgmental about these dramatic mood swings. She had long since (dating back to age nine) known, corresponded with, and directly spoken to Mother de Gonzague before she entered Carmel. But once enclosed behind the brick-and-mortar cloister, the tone and tenor of their relationship changed substantially. Given Mother de Gonzague's position as Prioress, such a shift was neither unexpected nor unacceptable. Her authority was required "to manage everyone's susceptibilities and obtain the calm necessary for respect of the rules, for prayer, and for contemplation."[2] Accordingly, the previous familiarity they both enjoyed was now altered by the normative standards their newfound roles—Prioress, Postulant—implied.

While on the one hand, Mother de Gonzague saw Thérèse as a "treasure," on the other hand "she kept herself from showing the slightest benevolence, thinking that severity was the only path to preserve this treasure."[3] Thérèse intuitively understood and accepted the nature of and necessity for this ambivalence:

"I know that she loved me very much…nevertheless, God permitted that she was VERY SEVERE without her even being aware of it…What an inestimable grace! How visibly God was acting within her who took His place! What would have become of me if I had been the 'pet' of the community as some of the Sisters believed?"[4]

With the passage of time and the accumulation of experience, Mother de Gonzague came to increasingly rely on Thérèse's good sense and spiritual maturity, entrusting her with the day-to-day task of running the novitiate and assigning to her the care of a second spiritual brother, Adolphe Roulland. In fact, Mother de Gonzague went so far as to describe Thérèse as both a "mystic" and a "comic," as someone who "can make you weep with devotion and just as easily faint with laughing during recreation."[5] It would appear, then, that "at the last a relationship of unclouded friendship prevailed between the two of them."[6]

THE CROSS IS OUR LOT
[Adapted From the Letters of Mother de Gonzague to Thérèse]

Earth: a desert not made to delight the exiled.
Suffering: the way Jesus treats His privileged.
He leads us to Tabor, but more often to Calvary.

How good it is to enjoy the absence of joys.
In these privations, we discover a gold mine
That will increase a hundredfold.

A very little humiliation, well-received, accepted
With joy, is worth more to the divine Master than
All the greatest Crosses of the world!

Faults make our life a meritorious life, an apostolic
Life; victories won over our faults obtain all we
Desire: souls for Jesus.

As for miseries, we must form a little package out
Of them and place it in the Heart of Jesus; He will
Change them into merits for the homeland.

In order to rejoice together, let us suffer together:
The sacrifice, the immolation of our most cherished
Desires, the giving of our entire self.

Let us be saints, but not made by false devotion.
Let us love Jesus, let us live by love in order to
Die from love.

Marie of the Angels

10

MARIE OF THE ANGELS
(1845–1924)

Sister Marie of the Angels and the Sacred Heart spent the better part of six decades behind the cloistered walls of the Lisieux Carmel. During her tenure she twice held the titles of Subprioress (1883–1886; 1893–1899) and Mistress of Novices (1886–1893; 1897–1909). It was in this latter office that she became one of Thérèse's formation directors.

Regarding her character, Thérèse described Sister Marie of the Angels as "a saint, the finished product of the first Carmelites."[1] But Thérèse was less favorably disposed to her Novice Mistress' manner of spiritual guidance, claiming that though "her kindness toward me was limitless...my soul did not expand under her direction."[2] On balance, however, and in fairness to Sister Marie of the Angels, it should be noted that Thérèse herself acknowledged many times over that Jesus alone was her "Director of directors."[3] This notwithstanding, Thérèse was obedient to a fault in judiciously heeding the dictates of her superiors as the sacrosanct word of God Himself. Even Sister Marie of the Angels conceded in her testimony at the diocesan tribunal that Thérèse "saw only God in authority; the ciborium might be of gold or copper, but it was always to our Lord that she paid her respect, her love and her obedience—in a word, her faith."[4] In further acknowledging the amiable, if heroic, esteem with which she held Thérèse, Sister Marie of the Angels noted, "She was an angel in a human body. Never did the slightest careless word cross her lips…Her purity was reflected in her heavenly expression, always so calm, so kindly, and so dignified."[5]

In the rhythmic nature of life, events and relationships often come full circle. Such was the case between Thérèse and Sister Marie of the Angels: as the former grew in "grace and wisdom,"[6] the latter solicited her "extraordinary insight into religious perfection."[7] This solicitation was not solely posthumous, as we learn firsthand in her deposition testimony: "With exquisite charity Sister Thérèse of the Child Jesus comforted me during many difficulties that I encountered and that she sensed were so painful to me."[8] Moreover, according to Mother Agnes of Jesus, "these two saints…encouraged each other mutually to valiantly bear the battles of the Lord and to sacrifice themselves entirely to save souls."[9] After Thérèse's death, Sister Marie of the Angels kept a notebook entitled "Smiles From My Little Thérèse," in which she recorded the many personal favors she received. This devotion continued right up until her death on November 24, 1924, just a few months shy of Thérèse's Canonization.

RETURN TO SENDER

[Adapted From the Letters of Sister Marie of the Angels to Thérèse]

Let the Child Jesus play games with
His very dear and precious little ball.
Smile at Him still, smile at Him always.
The more He makes you suffer,
The more you are to love Him!
Let everything in your soul sing
The intoxicating songs of Calvary.

Jesus does not will any joys to
His little grain of dust.
This is a grace par excellence.
Attach yourself to the Cross like ivy.
May divine suffering be your life.
Plunge into this bottomless ocean;
There alone are life and happiness.

Jesus loves you with predilection.
Love Jesus in suffering for Jesus!
May this sublime poverty be
Your whole ambition, your joy!
Make yourself more and more
A little victim, the holocaust of Jesus.
Nothing will escape His loving gaze!

Aid Jesus in extending His kingdom.
Save souls by your sacrifices;
Many will owe their heaven to you,
A real Carmelite of the desert.
Your way is pleasing to Him: to be nothing,
To feel nothing, to love nothing in yourself
So as to find everything in Jesus.

Take flight to the All of your heart
With wings of humility, simplicity, love.
Always love to be little, to be unseen by
All in order to be seen by God alone.
What does it matter if your heart is little,
Provided your desires are great!
His crown awaits you; refuse Him nothing!

Marie of the Trinity

11

MARIE OF THE TRINITY
(1874–1944)

Forced to leave the Carmel of Paris because of pressing health concerns after a two-year stint (1891–1893), Sister Marie of the Trinity entered the Lisieux Carmel in 1894. Mother Agnes of Jesus, then Prioress, designated Thérèse as her "angel," a customary practice equivalent to that of a mentor. As such, Thérèse was authorized to school Sister Marie of the Trinity in the traditions and Rule of the Order. Thérèse's tutelage, however, did not stop there. She was subsequently asked to assume the duties of novice mistress, absent the official title. It was in this role especially that Thérèse and Sister Marie of the Trinity forged what Father Pierre Descouvemont called a "transformative relationship."[1]

From the outset, Sister Marie of the Trinity was perceived by many of the nuns as "difficult and unruly,"[2] a "street urchin"[3] who "did not conform easily to the demands of community life."[4] In a letter to her sister Céline, Thérèse described her as a "wild rabbit," citing "her education [as] the cause of her unattractive ways."[5] Mother Agnes of Jesus somewhat euphemistically assessed her character as "independent," albeit "impulsive."[6] Despite these labels and abrasive traits, Thérèse saw in her a fundamental goodness and love of God that was at once childlike and faith-filled.

With grit and admonishment, passion and perseverance, Thérèse sought to instill in Sister Marie of the Trinity a devotion to both the charism of the Carmelites and the tenets of her "Little Way of Spiritual Childhood."[7] She was patently successful on both scores. To be sure, the half-century Sister Marie of the Trinity spent in the Lisieux monastery speaks to the authenticity of her vocation as a contemplative Carmelite. Moreover, to say that "she profited from the spiritual counsels of her novice mistress…and rapidly became her friend and ardent disciple"[8] cannot be overemphasized. In her own words, she humbly maintained, "My memories of Thérèse are sufficient for my prayers and I know that God does not ask anything else from me but to follow the 'Little Way' upon which Thérèse guided my first steps."[9] She remained steadfast to this resolution throughout the rest of her life.

In 1923, Sister Marie of the Trinity contracted Lupus, which continued to get progressively worse until her death. This disease "slowly disfigured her face and gave her the appearance of a 'leper.'"[10] Far from being disheartened by her condition, she thanked God for "the resemblance to the Sorrowful Face of His Son."[11] On the morning of January 16, 1944, "after a short agony,"[12] Sister Marie of the Trinity and the Holy Face succumbed to this disease. Her last words were: "In heaven I will follow little Thérèse everywhere."[13]

SPIRITUAL DIRECTION
[Adapted From the Letters of Thérèse to Sister Marie of the Trinity]

Beloved little spouse, do not be grieved!
You cannot play and smile except by
Suffering, by forgetting yourself.
Let the Sisters render you this service.
Be thankful to them: the most assiduous
In not letting you relent.

May the divine little Jesus find in your soul
An abode all perfumed with the roses of Love.
May He find there the burning lamp of fraternal
Charity, which will warm His little cold members
By making Him forget the ingratitude of souls
Who do not love Him enough.

Jesus gave you His Kiss of union which will be
Accomplished in heaven to the degree that you
Remain little and become more so each day.
Seek neither your own gain nor reward but to
Be despised through Love; this loss God will
Judge to be His gain in the evening of life!

Almire Pichon

12

ALMIRE PICHON
(1843–1919)

Tainted to some degree by the Jansenistic culture in which she was raised, Thérèse early on in her spiritual development, suffered occasional bouts of scrupulosity, believing her innocent thoughts and actions were sinful and offensive to God. Her more mature and overarching theology of seeing God through the decidedly optimistic lens of confidence and love was fortified during an encounter with Father Pichon.

Shortly after entering Carmel, and while still a postulant, Thérèse met Father Pichon for the first time. Already a spiritual advisor to the Martin sisters, he had come to witness the Profession of Sister Marie of the Sacred Heart. During his stay, Thérèse reviewed with him her life to date in the context of a general confession. Although she was initially hesitant to describe to him the state of her soul, courage prevailed. At the end of this reconciliation session, Thérèse had what surely could be classified as an epiphany moment. She recalled this event in her autobiography: "He spoke the most consoling words I ever heard in my life: 'In the presence of God, the Blessed Virgin, and all the Saints, I DECLARE THAT YOU HAVE NEVER COMMITTED A MORTAL SIN.'"[1] Thérèse was so moved by these words that she considered them as "coming from the mouth of Jesus Himself."[2]

After his departure, Father Pichon and Thérèse were never again to meet face to face, though they periodically corresponded with each other. Regrettably, Father Pichon did not keep any of the letters he received from Thérèse.

LITTLE TOY OF JESUS
[Adapted From the Letters of Father Pichon to Thérèse]

My dear Benjamin in Our Lord, there is
No ocean between your soul and mine.
There isn't even the point of a needle,
A thread of silk.
In the Heart of Jesus, there is union,
There is fusion.

Give God a free hand, for the school
Of Calvary is good.
It is there that the adorable Master
Fashions His disciples, molds His friends
According to His Heart, unites His
Little spouses to Himself.

God takes greater pleasure in the soul
Transformed by sorrow than by love.
Love all that comes to you from Jesus:
EVERYTHING, even the most bitter gall,
The sharpest thorns, your most filial
Agonies, the divine absences.

Be obstinate in smiling at Our Lord anyway.
It is better to love Jesus on His terms.
Take joy in being nothing since Jesus is all.
Bless God that you feel nothing, possess
Nothing, find nothing in yourself.
Rejoice to be of such little consequence.

Let the little lamb remain in its poverty
And let its misery be its hope.
Yearn to wipe the tears of Jesus; offer
To cry and to suffer in His stead.
Be consumed with the desire of possessing
Him, of loving Him to distraction.

To love here below is to suffer.
Let it not be enough for you to love Jesus,
You must make Him loved; otherwise, you
Would not be a daughter of St. Teresa.
How good it is to vow oneself to Him,
To sacrifice oneself for His love.

Carry out this ardent desire for sanctity,
For the apostolate.
Since everything is suffering and exile, be
Happy; enjoy your tête-à-tête with Jesus.
The angels and the saints envy you.
Your crown of thorns makes them jealous.

THE MASTER'S HERITAGE
[Adapted From the Letters of Father Pichon to Thérèse]

Little Lamb of the Child Jesus, may the thirst
Of being an apostle by aiding apostles increase
And develop more and more in your heart.
Live the martyrdom of the heart: the daily
Martyrdom of pinpricks.
Rejoice in being only a poor little nothing.
Profit from this great grace.

Jesus has given you His Childhood and His
Passion: what an incomparable dowry!
Seek and find your happiness in the
Bitterness of your divine Spouse.
Walk in humility; there only is He to be found.
Let Our Lord nourish you with the royal dish
Of His Gospel!

Take my word, dear Child of my soul, never
Have you committed a mortal sin!
You cannot sin gravely without knowing it.
You must not doubt your state of grace.
Banish your worries; God wills it, I command it!
Sleep in abandonment on God's Heart.
He will never betray you.

When your interior is tossed by the tempest,
Keep calm and serene in your exterior.
To be sure, this is a holy hypocrisy!
Kneel before the Tabernacle to thank Him: this is
Heaven before heaven, the heaven of heavens!
Long live peace, joy, confidence.
Always smile for the divine Spouse.

Maurice Bellière

13

MAURICE BELLIÈRE
(1874–1907)

During the Priorate of Mother Agnes of Jesus, Maurice Bellière, a twenty-one-year-old seminarian, wrote to the Lisieux Carmel asking for a spiritual sister who would devote herself to his salvation and obtain for him the grace to be faithful to the vocation of priest and missionary.[1] In selecting Thérèse, Mother Agnes ignited "a love between a man and a woman whose lives were given totally, in vowed celibacy, to God and to others."[2]

Though they never met, their holy friendship, as poignantly documented in their correspondence, spanned the final two years of Thérèse's life. For his part, Maurice shared with Thérèse his personal and apostolic hopes and desires, as well as his past regrets and uncertainties about his vocation. On her end, Thérèse spoke compassionately about God's unconditional love and humbly counseled him on the doctrine of her "Little Way."

Serendipitously, as if by providential design, Maurice departed for Africa on the very day Thérèse died. Although he was ordained by the Order of his choice, the White Fathers, in 1901, he unceremoniously withdrew from his assigned mission and returned to France in 1905 without official authorization. Shortly thereafter, he left the White Fathers, evidently of his own accord. From that point forward, Maurice's mental state—perhaps exacerbated by both the death of his mother[3] and the presumed infection of sleeping sickness—deteriorated so rapidly that he had to be institutionalized at Bon Sauveur in Caen, where, at the age of thirty-three, he died in 1907.[4]

THE HIDDEN MANNA TO THE VICTOR
[Adapted From the Letters of Thérèse to Maurice Bellière]

The Strong God is treating you as a privileged one.
He wills that you save souls through suffering.
Your mission, your lot is beautiful: martyrdom
Of the heart and of blood; both are worthy of an
Apostle of Christ.

Let us work together for the salvation of souls.
We have only the one day of this life to save them.
The tomorrow of this day will be eternity.
Through prayer and suffering let us remain close
To the crib of Jesus.

Like brother and sister, a good missionary, a poor
Carmelite, our souls are made to understand each other:
Equally endowed with spiritual goods, submitting to Him
The kingdom of hearts, working solely for His glory, doing
Nothing for self or for creatures.

Since we are now two the work will be done more quickly.
Suffering united to love is the only way to merit heaven.
Your soul is the sister to my own, called not to climb
The rough stairway of fear but to raise itself up to God
By the ELEVATOR of love.

Familiarity with Jesus seems difficult for you to realize.
When I am delivered from my mortal envelope, I shall
Be sure to help you walk by this delightful way.
Instead of losing me, you will find me.
I am not your little sister for nothing.

The way of simple and loving confidence is made for you.
Our Savior has long since forgotten your infidelities.
Only your desires for perfection give joy to His Heart.
For those who love Him and who come after each indelicacy
To ask pardon, Jesus is thrilled with joy.

I beg you, do not to drag yourself to His feet but follow that
Impulse which draws you where your place is: into His arms.
With entire filial confidence, cast your mortal faults into the
Devouring fire of Love, and soon, like St. Augustine, you will
Say: "Love is the weight that draws me."

THE BREEZE FROM THE CARMEL
[Adapted From the Letters of Maurice Bellière to Thérèse]

The missionary must be a saint, and I am not one.
More than anyone else I have to make reparation.
I need all God's grace: the virtue of the strong,
Beautiful abnegation, zeal for His glory, humility
Which is the foundation of sanctity.

My soul and work are entrusted to your solicitude.
Pray that the Master bring about some progress in me.
I have to break myself away from great affections,
Cherished habits of easy living, a happy past that still
Strongly attracts me.

Your poor brother would like to sing like you, but He,
Who is all good, grants me only my rough and ready prose.
I have to make God forget my sinful past by real penance;
And, then, to work in His vineyard.
Beg God, the Mediator between our souls, that I die a martyr!

My chosen career: the White Fathers' African Missions.
You will not be the least support for my poor soul.
May confidence prevail so I can give myself without reservations.
Since we are two at work, I rely fully on the Lord and on you.
I consider, as coming from Jesus Himself, all that you say to me.

You open up new horizons for me: on the mercy of Jesus,
On the familiarity He encourages, on the simplicity of the
Soul's relations with this Great God.

Since you understand me, make me generous, irreproachable
To Jesus.

You are about to leave—what a blow to my poor heart.
I was depending on making a sweet habit of your holy intimacy,
And I was consoled, strengthened, and uplifted by the one
Whom Jesus had lent it as an angel on earth.
Now Jesus withdraws this good—how painful for my shallow soul.

Leave little Sister, do not make Jesus wait any longer.
Let me battle on, carry the cross, fall beneath it, and
Die in pain; you will be here just the same.
You will be my pilot, you will win my case, and draw me to
Him on the last day, for without you I cannot even stand.

The Master is teaching me to detach myself from everything
That is passing and to look only at Him.
In the union of our apostolate and love for Jesus, obtain
Suffering for me so that I may be separated from you the
Least possible in heaven.

No doubt Jesus is the Treasure, but I found Him in you, and
He was more approachable.
My heart found yours in our mutual Friend, and it is still by
Means of you that He will come to me.
From Heaven as from here below, I expect ALL from you.

Adolphe Roulland

14

ADOLPHE ROULLAND
(1870–1934)

In late May 1896, Adolphe Roulland, then a missionary aspirant, wrote to Mother Marie de Gonzague, Prioress of the Lisieux Carmel, requesting that a nun be assigned to pray specifically for him and for the success of his impending apostolate. She chose Thérèse to assume this role. Adolphe Roulland was to become Thérèse's second spiritual brother. A short month later, on June 28, he was ordained a priest of the Paris Society of Foreign Missions. Five days thereafter, he said his first Mass at the Lisieux Carmel, where he met and twice spoke with Thérèse. Within the space of a month, he set sail for China.

Over the course of the next year, he and Thérèse exchanged a half dozen letters. Responding to the first letter of her newly acquired spiritual brother, Thérèse penned these reassuring words: "When the ocean will separate you from France, you will recall… that on the mountain of Carmel a soul is praying unceasingly to the divine Prisoner of Love for the success of your glorious conquest."[1]

After her death, and in defense of her cause for beatification, Father Roulland offered the following testimony: "I see from her letters that she really saw nothing but God and desired nothing but God as a result of a pure and absolutely disinterested love… It is precisely because she never lost sight of this pure love that her virtue appears heroic to me…I unhesitatingly attribute a great number of spiritual blessings to her intercession."[2]

APOSTOLIC UNION IN THE HEART OF CHINA
[Adapted From the Letters of Father Adolphe Roulland to Thérèse]

Am I not in some way a child of Carmel?
Have I not for a sister in Jesus a daughter of St. Teresa?
Our apostolate, yours and mine, will be blessed by God
On the mountain of Carmel; there, a soul will be praying
For the success of him who will be fighting in the field.

Like that of a Carmelite, a missionary's life is accompanied
By sufferings; these crosses I will carry with a smile if I
Remain faithful to the traditions of my forebears.
Without the cross and suffering, I shall do nothing for the
Glory of God and the salvation of souls.

I have reached my country of adoption: the soil of China.
I am confident in the future because it is God's and
Because in Carmel a Sister will pray for me.
Together, we shall convert souls, we shall baptize babies.
These angels will owe their eternal happiness to you.

My sorrows, my joys, these I will tell you; we shall weep
And rejoice together when you fly away to the homeland.
In spirit I shall at times be in your chapel.
Perhaps we shall meet together at the Master's feet,
Praying for our sanctification and that of souls.

In Apostolic union I need your prayers today, tomorrow,
And the rest of my life!
If bandits kill me and I am not worthy to enter heaven
Immediately, you will draw me out of purgatory, and
I shall go to await you in paradise.

THE SOUL OF A MISSIONARY
[Adapted From the Letters of Thérèse to Father Adolphe Roulland]

The God of Goodness willed to realize my dream:
To work with you for the salvation of souls!
For this purpose I became a Carmelite.
I feel unworthy of being united to you, one of
The missionaries of our adorable Jesus, by the
Apostolic bonds of prayer and mortification.

Since obedience trusts me with this sweet task, my
Heavenly Spouse will make up for my feeble merits.
He uses the weakest instruments to work marvels!
When the ocean will separate you from France, recall
That on the mountain of Carmel, a soul is praying
Unceasingly to the divine Prisoner of Love for your success.

Your sword is that of the word and apostolic works.
After having given Jesus love for love, life for life,
You will give Him blood for blood: martyrdom!
Only then will you resemble Him, taking on the form
And nature of a slave, becoming like one of us in order
To redeem our souls for eternity.

My only weapon is suffering which is sweet when
Embraced for the love of Jesus Christ.
Joy sought and tested in works and suffering is a
Foretaste of the happiness of heaven.
To be truly happy we must suffer, and to live we must die!
This paradise is that of the missionary and the Carmelite.

You seem to doubt your immediate entrance into heaven.
Save the Immaculate Virgin, no human life is exempt
From faults; thus, my way is all confidence and love.
I expect as much from God's justice as from His mercy.
It is sufficient to recognize one's nothingness and to
Abandon oneself as a child into God's arms.

Soon I shall sit down at the heavenly banquet.
I will ask the Ocean of Love without shores the
Palm of martyrdom for you; I shall hold your hand and
Help you gather this glorious palm without effort.
Then, we shall fly together into the heavenly homeland,
Surrounded by all the souls who will be your conquest!

Thérèse offers a mature synthesis of Christian spirituality: she combines theology and the spiritual life; she expresses herself with strength and authority, with a great ability to persuade and communicate, as is shown by the reception and dissemination of her message among the People of God. Thérèse's teaching expresses with coherence and harmonious unity the dogmas of the Christian faith as a doctrine of truth and an experience of life... The core of her message is actually the mystery itself of God-Love, of the Triune God, infinitely perfect in Himself... Thérèse possesses an exceptional universality. Her person, the Gospel message of the "little way" of trust and spiritual childhood have received and continue to receive a remarkable welcome, which has transcended every border.

Pope Saint John Paul II, Apostolic Letter, *Divini Amoris Scientia*

APPENDICES

APPENDIX A
THE POEMS: BY HISTORICAL PERIOD(S)
According to the stages of Thérèse's life
(See "Organizational Structure")

Poems are listed in alphabetical order.

1. A Faithful Echo: Fifth Period
2. A Martin Original: Fifth Period
3. A Moment Between Two Eternities: Fourth Period
4. Apostolic Union in the Heart of China: Seventh Period
5. Contemplating Immensity: Fourth Period
6. Crossing the Finish Line: Seventh Period
7. Dream Whisperer: Sixth Period
8. Eternal Espousals: Third Period
9. Familial Gratitude: Fourth through Seventh Periods
10. Hither and Yon: Seventh Period
11. Homeward Bound: Fourth Period
12. In Anticipation: Fourth Period
13. Indivisible: Third Period
14. In God's Good Time: Second Period
15. Jesus' Predilection: Sixth Period
16. Jesus-Victim, Your Spouse and Mine: Sixth and Seventh Periods
17. Juxtaposition: Fourth Period
18. Knock, Knock: Third Period
19. Like Mother, Like Daughter: Third Period
20. Little Toy of Jesus: Third and Fourth Periods
21. Love Always Wins: Fourth Period
22. Maternal Intercession: First Period

23. Maternal Surrogate: Third through Seventh Periods
24. Midday: Sixth Period
25. My Incomparable King: Third Period
26. No Pain, No Gain: Second Period
27. Not as the World Gives: Sixth Period
28. Priceless: Seventh Period
29. Rescued at Sea: Sixth Period
30. Return to Sender: Third through Fifth Periods
31. RSVP: Second, Fifth, and Sixth Periods
32. Separation Anxiety: Third Period
33. Sisters Twice Over: Third Period
34. Sojourn: Fourth Period
35. Spiritual Direction: Seventh Period
36. Spiritual Twinship: Fifth Period
37. Stalled: Fifth Period
38. String of Pearls: Fourth Period
39. Swan Song: Seventh Period
40. The Breeze from the Carmel: Seventh Period
41. The Cross Is Our Lot: Third, Fifth, and Sixth Periods
42. The Eucharistic Jesus: First Period
43. The Hidden Manna to the Victor: Seventh Period
44. The Marriage Contract: Sixth Period
45. The Master's Heritage: Fifth and Sixth Periods
46. The Soul of a Missionary: Seventh Period
47. The Time Is at Hand: Seventh Period
48. Theology 101: Seventh Period
49. True Devotee: Second, Sixth, and Seventh Periods
50. Twenty-Fourth Floor, Going Up: Seventh Period
51. When All Is Said and Done: Second Period

APPENDIX B
THE POEMS: VERSE ATTRIBUTION BY LETTER

Poems are listed in alphabetical order.

With the exception of a few archival references from the Lisieux Carmel, all cited material comes from the *General Correspondence, Volumes I and II* (Centenary Edition, ICS Publications). For cross-referencing purposes, the abbreviations used therein have been retained as follows:

LT (Letters from Thérèse)
LC (Letters from Thérèse's Correspondents)
LD (Diverse letters from the Correspondents)
ACL (Lisieux Carmel Archives)[1]

Additionally, in keeping with the rules of grammar and stylistic composition, the original correspondence has in some instances been altered to suit its new framework. These alterations are designated by the abbreviations listed below:

T (Tense)
P (Pronoun)
N (Number)
D (Diction)
S (Syntax)

A FAITHFUL ECHO
Title: LT 129

Stanza One
V1: LT 122
V2: LT 122
V3: LT 122, D
V4: LT 122
V5: LT 122

Stanza Two
V1: LT 122
V2: LT 122
V3: LT 122, D
V4: LT 122
V5: LT 122

Stanza Three
V1: LT 126
V2: LT 126
V3: LT 126
V4: LT 126
V5: LT 126

Stanza Four
V1: LT 127
V2: LT 127
V3: LT 127, LT 129
V4: LT 129, LT 130
V5: LT 130

Stanza Five
V1: LT 130
V2: LT 130, D
V3: LT 130
V4: LT 130, S
V5: LT 130

Stanza Six
V1: LT 130, S
V2: LT 130
V3: LT 130
V4: LT 127
V5: LT 137

A MARTIN ORIGINAL
Title: Original

Stanza One
V1: LT 124
V2: LT 124
V3: LT 124, D
V4: LT 124, LT 132

Stanza Two
V1: LT 124
V2: LT 124
V3: LT 132
V4: LT 132

Stanza Three
V1: LT 132
V2: LT 132
V3: LT 124
V4. LT 124

Stanza Four
V1: LT 124
V2: LT 124
V3: LT 132, S, N
V4: LT 132, D

Stanza Five
V1: LT 127
V2: LT 127
V3: LT 127, LT 132
V4: LT 132, D

A MOMENT BETWEEN TWO ETERNITIES
Title: LT 87

Stanza One
V1: LT 82
V2: LT 82
V3: LT 82, LT 81
V4: LT 81
V5: LT 81
V6: LT 83
V7: LT 83
V8: LT 83

Stanza Four
V1: LT 87, D
V2: LT 87
V3: LT 87
V4: LT 82
V5: LT 82
V6: LT 94
V7: LT 94
V8: LT 82

Stanza Two
V1: LT 83
V2: LT 83
V3: LT 83
V4: LT 85
V5: LT 85
V6: LT 85
V7: LT 85
V8: LT 85, D

Stanza Five
V1: LT 105, S, D
V2: LT 105, S, D
V3: LT 96, S, D
V4: LT 94
V5: LT 98, D
V6: LT 98
V7: LT 105
V8: LT 105, D

Stanza Three
V1: LT 85
V2: LT 85
V3: LT 85
V4: LT 85
V5: LT 81
V6: LT 89, LT 86
V7: LT 86, D
V8: LT 96

APOSTOLIC UNION IN THE HEART OF CHINA
Title: Original

Stanza One
V1: LC 165
V2: LC 165
V3: LC 165
V4: LC 165, D
V5: LC 165

Stanza Two
V1: LC 167, S
V2: LC 167, S
V3: LC 167, S
V4: LC 173
V5: LC 173

Stanza Three
V1: LC 171
V2: LC 171, D
V3: LC 171
V4: LC 171, D
V5: LC 171

Stanza Four
V1: LC 167
V2: LC 167, LC 171, D
V3: LC 173
V4: LC 173
V5: LC 173

Stanza Five
V1: LC 166
V2: LC 166
V3: LC 175
V4: LC 175
V5: LC 175

CONTEMPLATING IMMENSITY
Title: LC 129

Stanza One
V1: LC 129, LD (3-1-1889)
V2: LD (3-1-1889)
V3: LC 110
V4: LC 110
V5: LC 110

Stanza Four
V1: LD (7-22-1890)
V2: LD (7-22-1890)
V3: LD (3-4-1889), LD (3-1-1889), D
V4: LD (7-22-1890)
V5: LD (7-22-1890)

Stanza Two
V1: LC 110
V2: LC 110
V3: LC 110
V4: LC 110
V5: LC 110

Stanza Five
V1: LC 129
V2: LC 129
V3: LC 129, N
V4: LC 129, S
V5: LC 129

Stanza Three
V1: LD (7-22-1890), N
V2: LD (7-22-1890)
V3: LD (7-22-1890)
V4: LD (7-22-1890), N
V5: LD (7-22-1890), S

CROSSING THE FINISH LINE
Title: Original

Stanza One

V1: LT 211

V2: LT 211

V3: LT 211

V4: LT 211

V5: LT 211

V6: LT 211

Stanza Two

V1: LT 243, P, N

V2: LT 243, D

V3: LT 243, D

V4: LT 243, LT 259, D

V5: LT 259, D, P

V6: LT 259

Stanza Three

V1: LT 243, D

V2: LT 243, D, T

V3: LT 243

V4: LT 243, P, N

V5: LT 243, S, D, P

V6: LT 243, D, P

Stanza Four

V1: LT 245, D, P

V2: LT 245

V3: LT 245, LT 243, D, P, N

V4: LT 243, LT 227, P

V5: LT 227

V6: LT 227

DREAM WHISPERER
Title: Original

Stanza One
V1: LT 156, D
V2: LT 156
V3: LT 156
V4: LT 156

Stanza Two
V1: LT 156, S, D
V2: LT 156
V3: LT 156, D
V4: LT 156

Stanza Three
V1: LT 156, D
V2: LT 156
V3: LT 156, LT
140, S, D
V4: LT 156

Stanza Four
V1: LT 140
V2: LT 140, T
V3: LT 140, S, D, T
V4: LT 140

Stanza Five
V1: LT 140
V2: LT 140, S, P, T
V3: LT 140, S, D
V4: LT 140, D

Stanza Six
V1: LT 140, D, T
V2: LT 140, P
V3: LT 140, D, T
V4: LT 140, P

Stanza Seven
V1: LT 140, LT 156, S, D, P
V2: LT 156
V3: LT 156

V4: LT 156

Stanza Eight
V1: LT 156
V2: LT 156, D
V3: LT 156, D
V4: LT 156

Stanza Nine
V1: LT 156
V2: LT 156
V3: LT 156, S
V4: LT 156

ETERNAL ESPOUSALS
Title: Original

Stanza One
V1: LC 105, N
V2: LC 105, N
V3: LC 105, S
V4: LC 105, S, D

Stanza Four
V1: LC 100
V2: LC 100
V3: LC 100
V4: LC 100

Stanza Two
V1: LC 85
V2: LC 85
V3: LC 85
V4: LC 85

Stanza Five
V1: LC 83, LC 105, D
V2: LC 102, D
V3: LC 102, S
V4: LC 102, D

Stanza Three
V1: LC 100, D
V2: LC 100, D
V3: LC 100, LC 105, D
V4: LC 100

FAMILIAL GRATITUDE
Title: Original

Stanza One	Stanza Five
V1: LT 260, S	V1: LT 155, P
V2: LT 260, S	V2: LT 155, P
V3: LT 100, P	V3: LT 155
V4: LT 100, D	V4: LT 155

Stanza Two	Stanza Six
V1: LT 139, P	V1: LT 155
V2: LT 139, S	V2: LT 155
V3: LT 139, P	V3: LT 255, P, S, D
V4: LT 139, P	V4: LT 255, P

Stanza Three	Stanza Seven
V1: LT 139, P	V1: LT 255
V2: LT 139, P	V2: LT 255, P, S
V3: LT 139, P	V3: LT 255, P, S
V4: LT 139	V4: LT 255, P

Stanza Four	Stanza Eight
V1: LT 139	V1: LT 255, P, S
V2: LT 139	V2: LT 255, P, D
V3: LT 139	V3: LT 255, D, P
V4: LT 139	V4: LT 255, LT 155, D

HITHER AND YON
Title: Original

Stanza One	Stanza Two
V1: LC 192	V1: LC 195, S
V2: LC 192, S	V2: LC 195, S, D
V3: LC 192, S, D	V3: LC 195, S, D
V4: LC 192, S	V4: LC 195, S. D
V5: LC 192, LC 195, S	V5: LC 195, S, D
V6: LC 195, S, D	V6: LC 195, S, D
V7: LC 195, S, D	V7: LC 195
V8: LC 195	V8: LC 195
V9: LC 195	V9: LC 195
V10: LC 195, S, N	V10: LC 195
V11: LC 195, S, D	V11: LC 195
V12: LC 195, S	V12: LC 195, S
V13: LC 195, D	V13: LC 195
V14: LC 195	V14: LC 195, N, P
V15: LC 195, D	V15: LC 195, S, N, P
V16: LC 195	V16: LC 195
V17: LC 195, S, D	V17: LC 195
V18: LC 195	V18: LC 195, S, D
V19: LC 195	V19: LC 195

HOMEWARD BOUND
Title: Original

Stanza One
V1: LC 127
V2: LC 127
V3: LC 127
V4: LC 127, N
V5: LC 127

Stanza Two
V1: LC 127
V2: LC 127
V3: LC 127
V4: LC 115, S, D
V5: LC 127, D

Stanza Three
V1: LC 137
V2: LC 137, N
V3: LC 137
V4: LC 137
V5: LC 137

Stanza Four
V1: LC 137
V2: LC 137
V3: LC 137
V4: LC 137
V5: LC 137, D

Stanza Five
V1: LC 127
V2: LC 115
V3: LC 127
V4: LC 127
V5: LC 127

IN ANTICIPATION
Title: Original

Stanza One
V1: LC 112
V2: LC 112
V3: LC 112
V4: LC 112

Stanza Four
V1: LC 135
V2: LC 135, D
V3: LC 135
V4: LC 135

Stanza Seven
V1: LC 133
V2: LC 133, S
V3: LC 133
V4: LC 133, S, D

Stanza Two
V1: LC 112, S
V2: LC 112, S
V3: LC 112, N
V4: Picture, 9-8-1890

Stanza Five
V1: LC 135
V2: LC 135
V3: LC 135
V4: LC 135

Stanza Eight
V1: LC 133, S, D
V2: LC 133
V3: LC 133
V4: LC 133

Stanza Three
V1: LC 135
V2: LC 135
V3: LC 135, D
V4: LC 135

Stanza Six
V1: LC 142
V2: LC 142, S
V3: LC 142
V4: LC 142

Stanza Nine
V1: LC 133
V2: LC 133
V3: LC 133
V4: LC 133

Stanza Ten
V1: LC 133
V2: Picture, 9-8-1890, D
V3: Picture, 9-8-1890
V4: Picture, 9-8-1890

INDIVISIBLE
Title: Original

Stanza One
V1: LT 54
V2: LT 54, S
V3: LT 54, S
V4: LT 54

Stanza Two
V1: LT 74
V2: LT 74, LT 76
V3: LT 74
V4: LT 74

Stanza Three
V1: LT 76, D
V2: LT 76
V3: LT 55, S
V4: LT 55, LT 54, N

Stanza Four
V1: LT 55
V2: LT 55, D
V3: LT 55
V4: LT 54

Stanza Five
V1: LT 76, S
V2: LT 76
V3: LT 54, S, D
V4: LT 54, D

IN GOD'S GOOD TIME
Title: Original

Stanza One

V1: LT 43A

V2: LT 43A

V3: LT 43B, D

V4: LT 43B

V5: LT 43B, S, D

V6: LT 43B, S

Stanza Two

V1: LT 27

V2: LT 43B, S

V3: LT 43B, S

V4: LT 36, LT 27, D

V5: LT 27, LT 36

V6: LT 36, LT 27, D

Stanza Three

V1: LT 36

V2: LT 36, D

V3: LT 36

V4: LT 34

V5: LT 34, S, D

V6: LT 34

Stanza Four

V1: LT 36, S, D

V2: LT 36

V3: LT 27, D

V4: LT 27, D

V5: LT 27, D

V6: LT 27

Stanza Five

V1: LT 43B

V2: LT 43B

V3: LT 43B

V4: LT 22, D

V5: LT 36, S, D

V6: LT 36, S, D

JESUS' PREDILECTION
Title: LT 142

Stanza One
V1: LT 141, S, D
V2: LT 141, S, D
V3: LT 141, D
V4: LT 141
V5: LT 141
V6: LT 141

Stanza Two
V1: LT 141
V2: LT 141
V3: LT 141
V4: LT 141
V5: LT 141, S, D
V6: LT 141, S, D

Stanza Three
V1: LT 141
V2: LT 141
V3: LT 141, S, D
V4: LT 141
V5: LT 141, S, D
V6: LT 141

Stanza Four
V1: LT 141, D
V2: LT 141
V3: LT 141
V4: LT 141
V5: LT 141, D
V6: LT 141, D, T

Stanza Five
V1: LT 141
V2: LT 141
V3: LT 141, LT 142, D
V4: LT 142, LT 141
V5: LT 141, LT 147, D
V6: LT 147

JESUS-VICTIM, YOUR SPOUSE AND MINE
Title: LT 186

Stanza One

V1: LT 171, LT 191

V2: LT 191, LT 173, N

V3: LT 173, N

V4: LT 173, S, N

V5: LT 173

Stanza Four

V1: LT 170, LT 154

V2: LT 154, LT 176

V3: LT 164

V4: LT 158

V5: LT 158

Stanza Two

V1: LT 148, LT 173

V2: LT 163

V3: LT 163, P

V4: LT 257

V5: LT 257

Stanza Five

V1: LT 171, S, D

V2: LT 171, LT 257

V3: LT 148, S

V4: LT 148

V5: LT 148

Stanza Three

V1: LT 164

V2: LT 164

V3: LT 164

V4: LT 164, LT 191

V5: LT 191

Stanza Six

V1: LT 173, LT 170, S

V2: LT 173

V3: LT 173

V4: LT 186

V5: LT 186

JUXTAPOSITION
Title: Original

Stanza One
V1: LC 113, S
V2: LC 113, S
V3: LC 113, S

Stanza Two
V1: LC 113, S, D
V2: LC 113, D
V3: LC 113, S

Stanza Three
V1: LC 130, LC 113, N
V2: LC 130
V3: LC 130

Stanza Four
V1: LC 114
V2: LC 114
V3: LC 114, S, D

Stanza Five
V1: LC 114
V2: LC 114, S
V3: LC 114, LC 130, D

Stanza Six
V1: LC 114
V2: LC 114
V3: LC 114

Stanza Seven
V1: LC 130, S, D
V2: LC 130
V3: LC 113, S

Stanza Eight
V1: LC 113, D
V2: LC 113
V3: LC 113

Stanza Nine
V1: LC 130
V2: LC 130
V3: LC 130

Stanza Ten
V1: LC 114
V2: LC 114
V3: LC 114

Stanza Eleven
V1: LC 130
V2: LC 130
V3: LC 130

KNOCK, KNOCK
Title: LC 80

Stanza One
V1: LC 101, S, D
V2: LC 101, D
V3: LC 101
V4: LC 101

Stanza Four
V1: LC 101, S, D
V2: LC 101
V3: LC 101
V4: LC 101, D

Stanza Two
V1: LC 101
V2: LC 101
V3: LC 101
V4: LC 101

Stanza Five
V1: LC 106, D
V2: LC 107
V3: LC 107
V4: LC 107, D

Stanza Three
V1: LC 101
V2: LC 101
V3: LC 101, D
V4: LC 101

Stanza Six
V1: LC 101, LC, 107, D
V2: LC 107
V3: LC 106, D, N
V4: LC 106

LIKE MOTHER, LIKE DAUGHTER
Title: Original

Stanza One
V1: LT 49
V2: LT 49
V3: LT 49
V4: LT 75, D
V5: LT 75, D

Stanza Four
V1: LT 75
V2: LT 75
V3: LT 75, S, D
V4: LT 75
V5: LT 79

Stanza Two
V1: LT 79, S, D
V2: LT 79, LT 49, D
V3: LT 79, D
V4: LT 79
V5: LT 79

Stanza Five
V1: LT 79, LT 75, S, D
V2: LT 79, S, D
V3: LT 79, LT 75, D
V4: LT 49, LT 79
V5: LT 49, S, D

Stanza Three
V1: LT 79, LT 49, S, D
V2: LT 49, S, D
V3: LT 49, D
V4: LT 49, D
V5: LT 49, D

LITTLE TOY OF JESUS
Title: LC 97

Stanza One
V1: LC 97
V2: LC 97
V3: LC 97
V4: LC 97
V5: LC 97
V6: LC 97

Stanza Four
V1: LC 111
V2: LC 111
V3: LC 111
V4: LC 111
V5: LC 111
V6: LC 126

Stanza Seven
V1: LC 82, D, N
V2: LC 82
V3: LC 126, S
V4: LC 126, LC 108, S
V5: LC 132
V6: LC 132

Stanza Two
V1: LC 116, D
V2: LC 116
V3: LC 116
V4: LC 116
V5: LC 116
V6. LC 116

Stanza Five
V1: LC 116
V2: LC 116
V3: LC 117, D
V4: LC 117
V5: LC 87
V6. LC 87

Stanza Three
V1: LC 108
V2: LC 108
V3: LC 111
V4: LC 111
V5: LC 111
V6: LC 111

Stanza Six
V1: LC 117
V2: LC 126
V3: LC 126, D
V4: LC 126, S
V5: LC 108
V6: LC 108

LOVE ALWAYS WINS
Title: Original

Stanza One	**Stanza Five**	**Stanza Nine**
V1: LT 92, P	V1: LT 92	V1: LT 109
V2: LT 92	V2: LT 92	V2: LT 109
V3: LT 92, S	V3: LT 92	V3: LT 109

Stanza Two	**Stanza Six**	**Stanza Ten**
V1: LT 92	V1: LT 92	V1: LT 109, S
V2: LT 92	V2: LT 92	V2: LT 109, S, D
V3: LT 92	V3: LT 92	V3: LT 109

Stanza Three	**Stanza Seven**	**Stanza Eleven**
V1: LT 92	V1: LT 92, S	V1: LT 109, S, D
V2: LT 92	V2: LT 92	V2: LT 109, D
V3: LT 92, D	V3: LT 92	V3: LT 109, D

Stanza Four	**Stanza Eight**	**Stanza Twelve**
V1: LT 92	V1: LT 93	V1: LT 109, D
V2: LT 92	V2: LT 93	V2: LT 109, D
V3: LT 92	V3: LT 93	V3: LT 109

Stanza Thirteen
V1: LT 109, S, D
V2: LT 93, S, D
V3: LT 109, S, D

MATERNAL INTERCESSION
Title: Original

Stanza One
V1: LC 13, LC 11, T
V2: LC 13, S, D
V3: LC 13
V4: LC 13

Stanza Two
V1: LC 16, LC 18, D
V2: LC 16
V3: LC 16, LC 18, S, D, P
V4: LC 18, P

Stanza Three
V1: LC 12, D
V2: LC 12
V3: LC 13, LC 29, D, N
V4: LC 29

Stanza Four
V1: LC 8, S, D
V2: LC 8
V3: LC 4, S
V4: LC 4, D

MATERNAL SURROGATE
Title: Original

Stanza One
V1: LT 125
V2: LT 125
V3: LT 125, LT 138
V4: LT 138
V5: LT 138

Stanza Four
V1: LT 133
V2: LT 133
V3: LT 133
V4: LT 133, D
V5: LT 133, P

Stanza Seven
V1: LT 202, D
V2: LT 202, D
V3: LT 202, S
V4: LT 152, D, S
V5: LT 152, D, S

Stanza Two
V1: LT 125, P, N
V2: LT 125
V3: LT 125
V4: LT 125, P
V5: LT 125, LT 152, D

Stanza Five
V1: LT 71, S
V2: LT 71
V3: LT 71, LT 202, S, D
V4: LT 202, LT 99
V5: LT 99, N

Stanza Three
V1: LT 172
V2: LT 172, S
V3: LT 172
V4: LT 172, S, N
V5: LT 172, S

Stanza Six
V1: LT 202, D, S
V2: LT 202, D, S
V3: LT 152, D, S
V4: LT 152, D, S
V5: LT 152, D, S

MIDDAY
Title: LC 154

Stanza One
V1: LC 154
V2: LC 154, LC 159, D
V3: LC 159, P
V4: LC 159
V5: LC 154
V6: LC 152

Stanza Three
V1: LC 159, D
V2: LC 152
V3: LC 152
V4: LC 152, D
V5: LC 152, S, D, T
V6: LC 152, T

Stanza Two
V1: LC 154
V2: LC 154, D
V3: LC 159, D
V4: LC 159, S, D
V5: LC 159, S
V6: LC 159

Stanza Four
V1: Original
V2: LC 160
V3: LC 160
V4: LC 160, LC 154
V5: LC 154
V6: LC 154

MY INCOMPARABLE KING
Title: LT 77

Stanza One
V1: LT 68, LT 58
V2: LT 58, LT 46
V3: LT 46, LT 58
V4: LT 58
V5: LT 58, S

Stanza Four
V1: LT 68
V2: LT 68
V3: LT 61, S
V4: LT 61, S
V5: LT 61, D

Stanza Two
V1: LT 72, D
V2: LT 77, LT 72
V3: LT 72
V4: LT 72
V5: LT 72

Stanza Five
V1: LT 68
V2: LT 68
V3: LT 72
V4: LT 72
V5: LT 68, D

Stanza Three
V1: LT 68
V2: LT 68, D
V3: LT 68
V4: LT 68, S
V5: LT 68, S

Stanza Six
V1: LT 52
V2: LT 52, P
V3: LT 72, D
V4: LT 72
V5: LT 72

NO PAIN, NO GAIN
Title: Original

Stanza One
V1: LC 66

V2: LC 66, LC 57

V3: LC 57

V4: LC 57

Stanza Two
V1: LC 69

V2: LC 69

V3: LC 69

V4: LC 69

Stanza Three
V1: LC 64

V2: LC 64

V3: LC 64, LC 69

V4: LC 69

Stanza Four
V1: LC 78

V2: LC 78, S, P, N

V3: LC 78

V4: LC 78

Stanza Five
V1: LC 69

V2: LC 69

V3: LC 69

V4: LC 69

Stanza Six
V1: LD (11-8-1887), S

V2: LD (11-8-1887), LC 55

V3: LC 55

V4: LC 48

Stanza Seven
V1: LD (11-8-1887), S

V2: LD (11-8-1887), LC 48, S, D

V3: LC 78, P

V4: LC 66

Stanza Eight
V1: LC 76, D

V2: LC 76, S, D

V3: LC 64

V4: LC 64

NOT AS THE WORLD GIVES
Title: Original

Stanza One
V1: LT 142
V2: LT 142
V3: LT 142
V4: LT 142, S
V5: LT 142, D

Stanza Four
V1: LT 145
V2: LT 145
V3: LT 169, S
V4: LT 169, D
V5: LT 169, D

Stanza Two
V1: LT 142
V2: LT 142, D
V3: LT 142, D
V4: LT 142, S
V5: LT 142, S

Stanza Five
V1: LT 165, D
V2: LT 165, LT 169
V3: LT 169, D
V4: LT 145, S, D
V5: LT 145, LT 168, D

Stanza Three
V1: LT 143, S
V2: LT 143
V3: LT 143
V4: LT 145, LT 143, S
V5: LT 145

Stanza Six
V1: LT 157
V2: LT 157, LT 168, D
V3: LT 167, D
V4: LT 145
V5: LT 145

PRICELESS
Title: Original

Stanza One
V1: LC 169
V2: LC 169
V3: LC 169

Stanza Two
V1: LC 169
V2: LC 169
V3: LC 169

Stanza Three
V1: LC 169
V2: LC 169
V3: LC 169

Stanza Four
V1: LC 169
V2: LC 169, P
V3: LC 169, S

Stanza Five
V1: LC 170, P
V2: LC 170, S, D, P
V3: LC 170

Stanza Six
V1: LC 169, S, D
V2: LC 169, LC 170, S, D, T
V3: LC 169, D

Stanza Seven
V1: LC 169, D
V2: LC 170, S, D, T
V3: LC 170, D

RESCUED AT SEA
Title: Original

Stanza One
V1: LT 144, S
V2: LT 144
V3: LT 144
V4: LT 144
V5: LT 144

Stanza Two
V1: LT 144
V3: LT 144, D
V3: LT 144, D
V4: LT 144, D
V5: LT 144

Stanza Three
V1: LT 144, S, D
V2: LT 144
V3: LT 144, S, D, T
V4: LT 144, D
V5: LT 144, S, D

Stanza Four
V1: LT 144, D
V2: LT 144, D
V3: LT 144, D
V4: LT 144
V5: LT 144

Stanza Five
V1: LT 144, D
V2: LT 144, D
V3: LT 144, S
V4: LT 144, S, D
V5: LT 144

Stanza Six
V1: LT 144, D
V2: LT 144, D
V3: LT 144, D
V4: LT 144, D
V5: LT 144, D

Stanza Seven
V1: LT 157, D
V2: LT 157
V3: LT 157
V4: LT 157
V5: LT 157

RETURN TO SENDER
Title: Original

Stanza One

V1: LC 92, D

V2: LC 92, D

V3: LC 92

V4: LC 92

V5: LC 92

V6: LC 92

V7: LC 92

Stanza Two

V1: LC 120, D

V2: LC 119

V3: LC 120, D, S

V4: LC 119

V5: LC 119

V6: LC 119

V7: LC 119

Stanza Three

V1: LC 119

V2: LC 119

V3: LC 141, D

V4: LC 141

V5: LC 145

V6: LC 145

V7: LC 109

Stanza Four

V1: LC 109

V2: LC 109, D

V3: LC 145

V4: LC 145

V5: LC 145, LC 120, D

V6: LC 120

V7: LC 120, D, S

Stanza Five

V1: LC 119

V2: LC 119

V3: LC 119, D

V4: LC 119

V5: LC 104, P

V6: LC 104

V7: LC 109, P

RSVP
Title: Original

Stanza One

V1: LC 163

V2: LC 163, S, D
V3: LC 163, S, D

Stanza Two

V1: LC 163
V2: LC 163, S, D
V3: LC 163

Stanza Three

V1: LC 163, S, D

V2: LC 163, S

V3: LC 163, S

Stanza Four

V1: LC 68, S

V2: LC 68, S
V3: LC 68, S

Stanza Five

V1: LC 68, S
V2: LC 68, S, T
V3: LC 68

Stanza Six

V1: LD (11-17-1887), D

V2: LD (11-17-1887), S, D

V3: Original

Stanza Seven

V1: LD (11-17-1887), S, D

V2: LD (11-17-1887)

V3: LD (11-17-1887)

SEPARATION ANXIETY
Title: Original

Stanza One
V1: LC 88, LC 86
V2: LC 88
V3: LC 88, D
V4: LC 88

Stanza Two
V1: LC 86
V2: LC 86, S
V3: LC 88
V4: LC 88

Stanza Three
V1: LC 86, T
V2: LC 86
V3: LC 86, LC 96
V4: LC 96, LC 86, D

Stanza Four
V1: LC 96, LC 86
V2: LC 88, D
V3: LC 88, D, N
V4: LC 88

Stanza Five
V1: LC 86, D
V2: LC 88, N
V3: LC 86, D
V4: LC 86

SISTERS TWICE OVER
Title: Original

Stanza One
V1: LT 57, LT 47
V2: LT 47
V3: LT 65

Stanza Two
V1: LT 57, LT 53
V2: LT 53
V3: LT 53

Stanza Three
V1: LT 53
V2: LT 47, S
V3: LT 47, D

Stanza Four
V1: LT 57, D
V2: LT 57, S
V3: LT 57, D

Stanza Five
V1: LT 57
V2: LT 57
V3: LT 57

Stanza Six
V1: LT 65
V2: LT 65
V3: LT 65, S, D

Stanza Seven
V1: LT 57
V2: LT 57
V3: LT 57

Stanza Eight
V1: LT 57, S
V2: LT 57
V3: LT 57

SOJOURN
Title: Original

Stanza One
V1: LT 116
V2: LT 116
V3: LT 116, LT 91

Stanza Two
V1: LT 116
V2: LT 116
V3: LT 116

Stanza Three
V1: LT 116
V2: LT 116
V3: LT 116

Stanza Four
V1: LT 116, D
V2: LT 117
V3: LT 117

Stanza Five
V1: LT 111
V2: LT 111
V3: LT 111, D

Stanza Six
V1: LT 111, S, D
V2: LT 111, S
V3: LT 111, S

Stanza Seven
V1: LT 117
V2: LT 117
V3: LT 117

Stanza Eight
V1: LT 117
V2: LT 117, LT 91, D
V3: LT 91, D

SPIRITUAL DIRECTION
Title: Original

Stanza One
V1: LT 212, LT 236, S, D
V2: LT 212, T
V3: LT 212
V4: LT 212
V5: LT 212, S
V6: LT 212

Stanza Two
V1: LT 246
V2: LT 246
V3: LT 246
V4: LT 246
V5: LT 246
V6: LT 246

Stanza Three
V1: LT 187, D
V2: LT 187, D
V3: LT 242
V4: LT 188, S, D, P
V5: LT 188, S, D
V6: LT 188, T

SPIRITUAL TWINSHIP
Title: LT 134 (Introduction)

Stanza One	Stanza Four
V1: LT 134, S	V1: LT 134
V2: LT 134, S	V2: LT 134
V3: LT 134	V3: LT 134
V4: LT 134	V4: LT 134

Stanza Two	Stanza Five
V1: LT 134	V1: LT 135
V2: LT 134, D	V2: LT 137, S
V3: LT 134	V3: LT 137, S
V4: LT 134	V4: LT 137, S

Stanza Three	Stanza Six
V1: LT 134	V1: LT 137, D
V2: LT 134, S	V2: LT 135
V3: LT 134	V3: LT 135
V4: LT 134	V4: LT 135, S, D

STALLED
Title: Original

Stanza One
V1: LC 149, D
V2: LC 149
V3: LC 149
V4: LC 149

Stanza Four
V1: LC 149
V2: LC 149, S
V3: LC 149
V4: LC 149

Stanza Seven
V1: LC 149
V2: LC 149, D
V3: LC 149
V4: LC 149

Stanza Two
V1: LC 149, S, D
V2: LC 149
V3: LC 149
V4: LC 149

Stanza Five
V1: LC 149, S, D
V2: LC 149
V3: LC 149
V4: LC 149

Stanza Eight
V1: LC 149, S
V2: LC 149, S
V3: LC 149
V4: LC 149

Stanza Three
V1: LC 149, D
V2: LC 149
V3: LC 149
V4: LC 149

Stanza Six
V1: LC 149
V2: LC 149
V3: LC 149, S
V4: LC 149

STRING OF PEARLS
Title: Original

Stanza One
V1: LT 104
V2: LT 104
V3: LT 104

Stanza Two
V1: LT 114
V2: LT 114
V3: LT 114

Stanza Three
V1: LT 95
V2: LT 95
V3: LT 106

Stanza Four
V1: LT 115
V2: LT 115, S
V3: LT 115, LT 112, S, D

Stanza Five
V1: LT 112
V2: LT 110
V3: LT 115, D

Stanza Six
V1: LT 106
V2: LT 103, S, D
V3: LT 103, S

Stanza Seven
V1: LT 95, S
V2: LT 110, S
V3: LT 95, S

SWAN SONG
Title: LC 192

Stanza One	Stanza Two
V1: LC 192, S	V1: LC 192, S, D, T, P
V2: LC 192	V2: LC 192
V3: LC 192	V3: LC 192
V4: LC 192	V4: LC 192
V5: LC 192	V5: LC 192, D
V6: LC 192, S	V6: LC 192
V7: LC 192	V7: LC 195
V8: LC 192, S	V8: LC 195
V9: LC 192	V9: LC 195
V10: LC 192	V10: LC 195
V11: LC 192, S	V11: LC 195
V12: LC 192	V12: LC 192, N, P
V13: LC 192	V13: LC 192
V14: LC 192	V14: LC 192
V15: LC 192	V15: LC 192, S, D, P
V16: LC 192	V16: LC 192, S, P
V17: LC 192	V17: LC 192, S, D

THE BREEZE FROM THE CARMEL
Title: LC 177

Stanza One	**Stanza Four**	**Stanza Seven**
V1: LC 172	V1: LC 186, S, D	V1: LC 189
V2: LC 177	V2: LC 186	V2: LC 189
V3: LC 172	V3: LC 186, S, D	V3: LC 189
V4: LC 172	V4: LC 188, S	V4: LC 191, LC 189
V5: LC 172	V5: LC 188	V5: LC 189, LC 191

Stanza Two	**Stanza Five**	**Stanza Eight**
V1: LC 174	V1: LC 188	V1: LC 189
V2: LC 174	V2: LC 188	V2: LC 189
V3: LC 172	V3: LC 188	V3: LC 196, LC 191
V4: LC 172	V4: LC 191	V4: LC 191
V5: LC 172, S	V5: LC 191	V5: LC 191

Stanza Three	**Stanza Six**	**Stanza Nine**
V1: LC 174, S	V1: LC 189, S	V1: LC 193
V2: LC 174	V2: LC 189, D	V2: LC 193
V3: LC 177, S	V3: LC 189, S	V3: LC 193
V4: LC 177	V4: LC 189	V4: LC 193
V5: LC 177, S	V5: LC 189, D	V5: LC 193, D

THE CROSS IS OUR LOT
Title: LC 94

Stanza One
V1: LC 143, S
V2: LC 144, S, D
V3: LC 143, D

Stanza Four
V1: LC 144, S
V2: LC 144
V3: LC 144

Stanza Seven
V1: LC 162
V2: LC 144, S
V3: LC 144

Stanza Two
V1: LC 144
V2: LC 144, N
V3: LC 144

Stanza Five
V1: LC 94, D
V2: LC 94, D
V3: LC 94

Stanza Three
V1: LC 95
V2: LC 95, D
V3: LC 95

Stanza Six
V1: LC 144, S
V2: LC 103, S
V3: LC 103, S

THE EUCHARISTIC JESUS
Title: LC 24

Stanza One
V1: LC 22
V2: LC 22
V3: LC 22, S
V4: LC 22, S, D
V5: LC 22, LC 24, S, D

Stanza Two
V1: LC 23
V2: LC 23, D
V3: LC 23
V4: LC 21
V5: LC 21

Stanza Three
V1: LC 36
V2: LC 36
V3: LC 36
V4: LC 23, LC 25, S, D, N
V5: LC 25

Stanza Four
V1: LC 24
V2: LC 30, S, D
V3: LC 30, LC 31, S, D
V4: LC 30, LC 31, S, D
V5: LC 30, S, D

Stanza Five
V1: LC 36
V2: LC 36, D
V3: LC 36, LC 21
V4: LC 21
V5: LC 20

THE HIDDEN MANNA TO THE VICTOR
Title: LT 261

Stanza One
V1: LT 213
V2: LT 213, S
V3: LT 213
V4: LT 213, D
V5: LT 213

Stanza Two
V1: LT 213
V2: LT 213
V3: LT 213
V4: LT 213
V5: LT 213, S

Stanza Three
V1: LT 224, LT 198, LT 213
V2: LT 213, LT 220
V3: LT 220, LT 224, S, D
V4: LT 224, LT 244, S, D
V5: LT 244

Stanza Four
V1: LT 247, D
V2: LT 258, S, D
V3: LT 258, S
V4: LT 258, S
V5: LT 258

Stanza Five
V1: LT 258, D
V2: LT 258, S
V3: LT 258, S, D
V4: LT 258
V5: LT 261

Stanza Six
V1: LT 261
V2: LT 261, S, D
V3: LT 261
V4: LT 261, D
V5: LT 261

Stanza Seven
V1: LT 261, D
V2: LT 261, S
V3: LT 247, S, N
V4: LT 247, LT 258
V5: LT 258

THE MARRIAGE CONTRACT
Title: LT 183

Stanza One
V1: LT 183
V2: LT 183
V3: LT 183, S
V4: LT 183
V5: LT 183

Stanza Two
V1: LT 183
V2: LT 183
V3: LT 183
V4: LT 183
V5: LT 183

Stanza Three
V1: LT 183
V2: LT 183
V3: LT 183
V4: LT 183
V5: LT 183

Stanza Four
V1: LT 183
V2: LT 183
V3: LT 183, D
V4: LT 183, LT 165
V5: LT 165

Stanza Five
V1: LT 183
V2: LT 183
V3: LT 183
V4: LT 183
V5: LT 183

THE MASTER'S HERITAGE
Title: LC 158

Stanza One
V1: LC 151, LC 146
V2: LC 146
V3: LC 146
V4: LC 146
V5: LC 146
V6: LC 146
V7: LC 146, S

Stanza Three
V1: LC 151
V2: LC 151
V3: LC 151, N
V4: LC 151, N
V5: LC 151
V6: LC 161
V7: LC 151

Stanza Two
V1: LC 146
V2: LC 146
V3: LC 146, S
V4: LC 146
V5: LC 158, S, D
V6: LC 158, S
V7: LC 158, D

Stanza Four
V1: LC 146
V2: LC 146
V3: LC 146, D
V4: LC 151, LC 157, D
V5: LC 157
V6: LC 157
V7: LC 157

THE SOUL OF A MISSIONARY
Title: LT 201

Stanza One
V1: LT 189
V2: LT 189
V3: LT 189
V4: LT 189, S
V5: LT 189
V6: LT 189

Stanza Four
V1: LT 193, LT 221, S, D
V2: LT 221, D
V3: LT 221
V4: LT 221
V5: LT 226
V6: LT 221

Stanza Two
V1: LT 189
V2: LT 189
V3: LT 201
V4: LT 189
V5: LT 189, P
V6: LT 189

Stanza Five
V1: LT 226
V2: LT 226, S, D
V3: LT 226, D
V4: LT 226
V5: LT 226
V6: LT 226

Stanza Three
V1: LT 193
V2: LT 201
V3: LT 201, S
V4: LT 201, D
V5: LT 201
V6: LT 201

Stanza Six
V1: LT 254
V2: LT 254, S
V3: LT 254, S
V4: LT 254, S, D
V5: LT 254
V6: LT 254

THE TIME IS AT HAND
Title: Original

Stanza One
V1: LC 181
V2: LC 181
V3: LC 181
V4: LC 181
V5: LC 181

Stanza Two
V1: LC 183
V2: LC 183
V3: LC 183
V4: LC 183
V5: LC 183, D

Stanza Three
V1: LC 185
V2: LC 185, LC 183
V3: LC 183
V4: LC 185, S
V5: LC 185

Stanza Four
V1: LC 182
V2: LC 182, S
V3: LC 182, D
V4: LC 182, D
V5: LC 182

Stanza Five
V1: LC 185, D
V2: LC 185, D
V3: LC 185
V4: LC 185, D
V5: LC 185, D

THEOLOGY 101
Title: Original

Stanza One
V1: LT 196
V2: LT 196, D
V3: LT 196, D, P, N
V4: LT 196, D, P

Stanza Four
V1: LT 196, S
V2: LT 196, D
V3: LT 196
V4: LT 196, D

Stanza Two
V1: LT 196
V2: LT 196
V3: LT 196, LT 197
V4: LT 197

Stanza Five
V1: LT 197
V2: LT 197
V3: LT 197, LT 245, D
V4: LT 245

Stanza Three
V1: LT 196
V2: LT 196
V3: LT 196
V4: LT 196

Stanza Six
V1: LT 197
V2: LT 197, D
V3: LT 197, D, S
V4: LT 197, P

TRUE DEVOTEE
Title: Original

Stanza One
V1: LC 164, LC 156
V2: LC 156
V3: LC 164
V4: LC 56

Stanza Two
V1: LC 56, S, D
V2: LC 56
V3: LC 164, S
V4: LC 164, S

Stanza Three
V1: LC 50, LC 56
V2: LC 50, D
V3: LC 50
V4: LC 50

Stanza Four
V1: LC 56, LC 50
V2: LC 50
V3: LC 50
V4: LC 50

Stanza Five
V1: LC 56, S
V2: LC 56
V3: LC 56
V4: LC 56

Stanza Six
V1: LC 164, S, D
V2: LC 164
V3: LC 164
V4: LC 164

Stanza Seven
V1: LC 164, S, D
V2: LC 164
V3: LC 164, D
V4: LC 164, S, D

Stanza Eight
V1: LC 156
V2: LC 156
V3: ACL (5-8-1884)
V4: ACL (5-8-1884)

TWENTY-FOURTH FLOOR, GOING UP
Title: Original

Stanza One

V1: LT 230, D

V2: LT 230, D

V3: LT 230

V4: LT 230

Stanza Two

V1: LT 229

V2: LT 229

V3: LT 229

V4: LT 229

Stanza Three

V1: LT 216

V2: LT 216, D

V3: LT 216

V4: LT 216

Stanza Four

V1: LT 229

V2: LT 229

V3: LT 229

V4: LT 229

Stanza Five

V1: LT 245

V2: LT 245

V3: LT 245, D

V4: LT 245

WHEN ALL IS SAID AND DONE
Title: Original

Stanza One

V1: LC 70

V2: LC 70

V3: LC 70, LC 67, D

Stanza Two

V1: LC 70, T

V2: LC 70, D

V3: LC 70

Stanza Three

V1: LC 58, P

V2: LC 58

V3: LC 58

Stanza Four

V1: LD (11-20-1887)

V2: LC 70

V3: LC 70

Stanza Five

V1: LC 67

V2: LC 67

V3: LC 67

Stanza Six

V1: LC 67, S

V2: LC 67

V3: LC 61, P

Stanza Seven

V1: LC 67, N

V2: LC 67, LC 58, D

V3: LC 58, S

Notes

Introduction

1. Monica Prendergast, "Found Poetry as Literature Review: Research Poems on Audience and Performance," *Qualitative Inquiry* 12, no. 2 (April 2006), https://doi.org/10.1177/1077800405284601.

2. Academy of American Poets, https://poets.org.

3. Ibid.

4. John Clarke, OCD, trans., *General Correspondence, Vol. II* (Washington, DC: ICS Publications, 1988), 25.

5. Ibid., 5.

6. Ibid., 3.

7. Quoted in John Clarke, OCD, trans., *General Correspondence, Vol. I* (Washington, DC: ICS Publications, 1982), 53.

8. Ibid., 49–53.

9. Ibid., 49.

10. Clarke, *General Correspondence, Vol. I*, 75.

11. Quoted in Clarke, *General Correspondence, Vol. I*, 7.

12. Clarke, *General Correspondence, Vol. II*, LT 220, 1059.

13. Quoted in Donald Kinney, OCD, trans., *The Poetry of Saint Thérèse of Lisieux* (Washington, DC: ICS Publications, 1996), 18.

14. Kinney, *The Poetry of Saint Thérèse of Lisieux*, 11.

15. Ibid., 16.

16. Ibid.

17. Ibid., 7.

18. Ibid.

19. Ibid., 18.

Organizational Structure

1. Quoted in Clarke, *General Correspondence, Vol. I*, 43.

2. Clarke, *General Correspondence, Vol. I*, vi–vii. Clarke, *General Correspondence, Vol. II*, v–vi.

3. John Clarke, OCD, trans., *Story of a Soul: The Autobiography of St. Thérèse of Lisieux* (Washington, DC: ICS Publications, 1975), 245.

4. Clarke, *General Correspondence, Vol. I*, 94.

5. Ibid., 95.

6. Ibid.

7. Clarke, *General Correspondence, Vol. II*, 958.

8. Clarke, *General Correspondence, Vol. I*, 84.

9. Pierre Descouvement, *Thérèse of Lisieux and Marie of the Trinity: The Transformative Relationship of Saint Thérèse of Lisieux and Her Novice, Sister Marie of the Trinity* (Staten Island, NY: Alba House, 1997), xvii.

Chapter 1: Louis Martin

1. Quoted in Ida Friederike Görres, *The Hidden Face: A Study of St. Thérèse of Lisieux* (San Francisco, CA: Ignatius Press, 2003), 46.

2. Görres, *The Hidden Face*, 46.

3. Jean Chalon, *Thérèse of Lisieux: A Life of Love* (Liguori, MO: Liguori, 1997), 33.

4. Ibid., 34.

5. Clarke, *Story of a Soul*, 148.

6. Görres, *The Hidden Face*, 173.

7. Clarke, *Story of a Soul*, 148.

8. Dorothy Day, *Thérèse* (Springfield, IL: Templegate, 1960), 7.

Chapter 2: Pauline Martin

1. Day, *Thérèse*, 51.

2. Quoted in Görres, *The Hidden Face*, 44.

3. Görres, *The Hidden Face*, 44.

4. Chalon, *Thérèse of Lisieux*, 33.

5. Görres, *The Hidden Face*, 44.

6. Clarke, *Story of a Soul*, 44–45.

7. Ibid., 58.

8. Görres, *The Hidden Face*, 80.

9. Ibid.

10. Ibid.

11. Patricia O'Connor, *Thérèse of Lisieux: A Biography* (Huntington, IN: Our Sunday Visitor, 1983), 32.

12. Clarke, *Story of a Soul*, 148–49.

13. Archives of the Carmel of Lisieux, "Biography of Pauline (Mother Agnes) (1861–1951)," https://www.archives-carmel-lisieux.fr/english/carmel/index.php/chez-pauline/biography-of-pauline-mother-agnes.

14. Quoted in O'Connor, *Thérèse of Lisieux*, 61.

15. Clarke, *Story of a Soul*, 174.

16. Quoted in O'Connor, *Thérèse of Lisieux*, 89.

17. Clarke, *Story of a Soul*, 251.

18. Ibid.

19. Patrick Ahern, *Maurice and Thérèse: The Story of a Love* (New York: Doubleday, 1998), 12.

20. Christopher O'Mahony, OCD, ed. and trans., *St. Thérèse of Lisieux by Those Who Knew Her: Testimonies from the Process of Beatification* (Dublin, IE: Veritas, 1975), 33.

21. Clarke, *Story of a Soul*, xiii.

22. O'Mahony, *St. Thérèse of Lisieux by Those Who Knew Her*, 35.

23. Clarke, *Story of a Soul*, xv.

24. Görres, *The Hidden Face*, 24.

25. Clarke, *Story of a Soul*, xv.

26. Görres, *The Hidden Face*, 27.

27. O'Mahony, *St. Thérèse of Lisieux by Those Who Knew Her*, 36.

28. Day, *Thérèse*, 175.

29. Quoted in Görres, *The Hidden Face*, 387.

30. Ibid.

Chapter 3: Marie Martin

1. Quoted in Day, *Thérèse*, 46.

2. Day, *Thérèse*, 48.

3. Ibid., 47.

4. Quoted in Day, *Thérèse*, 49.

5. Görres, *The Hidden Face*, 93.

6. O'Connor, *Thérèse of Lisieux*, 22.

7. Clarke, *Story of Soul*, 67.

8. Ibid., 90.

9. Görres, *The Hidden Face*, 109.

10. Ibid., 124–125.

11. Ibid., 125.

12. Archives of the Carmel of Lisieux, "Biography of Marie of the Sacred Heart (1860–1940)," https://www.archives-carmel-lisieux.fr/english/carmel/index.php/marie-martin/biography-of-marie-of-the-sacred-heart.

13. Quoted in Görres, *The Hidden Face*, 143.

14. Archives of the Carmel of Lisieux, "Circular of Sister Marie of the Sacred Heart," https://www.archives-carmel-lisieux.fr/english/carmel/index.php/la-famille/marie-du-sacr%C3%A9-coeur/circulaire-de-marie-du-sacr%C3%A9-coeur.

15. Ibid.

16. Ibid.

Chapter 4: Céline Martin

1. Archives of the Carmel of Lisieux, "Circular of Sister Geneviève (Céline)," https://www.archives-carmel-lisieux.fr/english/carmel/index.php/la-famille/sr-genevi%C3%A8ve-c%C3%A9line/circulaire-de-sr-genevi%C3%A8ve-c%C3%A9line.

2. Quoted in Chalon, *Thérèse of Lisieux*, 21.

3. Clarke, *Story of a Soul*, 107.

4. Ibid., 103.

5. Archives of the Carmel of Lisieux, "Circular of Sister Geneviève (Céline)."

6. O'Mahony, *St. Thérèse of Lisieux by Those Who Knew Her*, 112.

7. Ibid., 115.

8. Ibid.

9 . Clarke, *Story of a Soul*, 106.

10. Ibid., 103–104.

11. Archives of the Carmel of Lisieux, "Circular of Sister Geneviève (Céline)."

12. Day, *Thérèse*, 61.

13. Clarke, *Story of a Soul*, 121.

14. Ibid., 134.

15. Ibid.

16. Ibid., 135.

17. Ibid., 136.

18. Archives of the Carmel of Lisieux, "Circular of Sister Geneviève (Céline)."

19. Quoted in *Thérèse of Lisieux*, 66.

20. Quoted in Chalon, *Thérèse of Lisieux*, 119.

21. Chalon, *Thérèse of Lisieux*, 122.

22. Clarke, *Story of Soul*, 177.

23. O'Mahony, *St. Thérèse of Lisieux by Those Who Knew Her*, 149.

24. Görres, *The Hidden Face*, 316.

25. Clarke, *Story of a Soul*, 177.

26. Chalon, *Thérèse of Lisieux*, 177.

27. Clarke, *Story of a Soul*, 177.

28. O'Connor, *Thérèse of Lisieux*, 90.

29. Clarke, *Story of a Soul*, 207.

30. Ibid., 207–208.

31. O'Mahony, *St. Thérèse of Lisieux by Those Who Knew Her*, 120.

32. Archives of the Carmel of Lisieux, "Circular of Sister Geneviève (Céline)."

33. Ibid.

34. O'Mahony, *St. Thérèse of Lisieux by Those Who Knew Her*, 159 and 161.

35. Chalon, *Thérèse of Lisieux*, 254.

36. O'Connor, *Thérèse of Lisieux*, 148.

37. Ibid.

38. Ibid., 148–149.

39. Ibid., 151.

40. Ibid., 150.

41. Archives of the Carmel of Lisieux, "Circular of Sister Geneviève (Céline)."

42. Ibid.

43. Ibid.

44. Ibid.

45. Ibid.

46. Ibid.

Chapter 5: Léonie Martin

1. Chalon, *Thérèse of Lisieux*, 26.
2. Day, *Thérèse*, 52.
3. Quoted in Day, *Thérèse*, 54.
4. Ibid., 58.
5. Quoted in *St. Thérèse of Lisieux by Those Who Knew Her*, 168.
6. O'Mahony, *St. Thérèse of Lisieux by Those Who Knew Her*, 168.
7. Archives of the Carmel of Lisieux, "Circular of Sister Françoise-Thérèse (Léonie Martin)," https://www.archives-carmel-lisieux.fr/english/carmel/index.php/chez-leonie/sr-fran%C3%A7oise-th%C3%A9r%C3%A8se-visitandine/circulaire-de-sr-fran%C3%A7oise-th%C3%A9r%C3%A8se.
8. Ibid.
9. Ibid.
10. Day, *Thérèse*, 61.

Chapter 6: Marie Guérin

1. Archives of the Carmel of Lisieux, "Circular of Sister Marie of the Eucharist (Marie Guérin)," https://www.archives-carmel-lisieux.fr/english/carmel/index.php/la-famille/marie-de-l-eucharistie-marie-gu%C3%A9rin/circulaire-de-marie-de-l-eucharistie-marie-gu%C3%A9rin.
2. Archives of the Carmel of Lisieux, "Biography of Marie Guérin (Marie of the Eucharist)," https://www.archives-carmel-lisieux.fr/english/carmel/index.php/chez-la-cousine-marie/bio-marie-guerin.
3. Quoted in Archives of the Carmel of Lisieux, "Circular of Sister Marie of the Eucharist (Marie Guérin)."
4. Archives of the Carmel of Lisieux, "Biography of Marie Guérin (Marie of the Eucharist)."

5. Ibid.

6. Quoted in Archives of the Carmel of Lisieux, "Circular of Sister Marie of the Eucharist (Marie Guérin)."

Chapter 7: Céline Guérin

1. Clarke, *Story of a Soul*, 35.

2. Ibid., 147.

3. Ibid., 35.

4. Clarke, *General Correspondence, Vol. I*, 361.

5. Clarke, *Story of a Soul*, 61.

6. Clarke, *General Correspondence, Vol. II*, 912.

Chapter 8: Isidore Guérin

1. Clarke, *Story of a Soul*, 42.

2. Guy Gaucher, *The Passion of Thérèse of Lisieux* (Chestnut Ridge, NY: Crossroad, 2000), 71.

3. O'Connor, *Thérèse of Lisieux*, 35.

4. Clarke, *General Correspondence, Vol. I*, 289.

5. Ibid., 296.

Chapter 9: Marie de Gonzague

1. Görres, *The Hidden Face*, 201.

2. Chalon, *Thérèse of Lisieux*, 117.

3. Ibid., 134–135.

4. Clarke, *Story of a Soul*, 150.

5. Quoted in O'Connor, *Thérèse of Lisieux*, 89.

6. Görres, *The Hidden Face*, 217.

Chapter 10: Marie of the Angels

1. Clarke, *Story of a Soul*, 151.

2. Ibid.

3. Ibid.

4. O'Mahony, *St. Thérèse of Lisieux by Those Who Knew Her*, 204.

5. Ibid., 211.

6. Ibid., 202.

7. Ibid., 203.

8. Archives of the Carmel of Lisieux, "Circular of Sister Marie of the Angels," https://www.archives-carmel-lisieux.fr/english/carmel/index.php/la-ma%C3%AEtresse-des-novices/marie-des-anges2/circulaire-marie-des-anges.

9. Ibid.

Chapter 11: Marie of the Trinity

1. Descouvement, *Thérèse of Lisieux and Marie of the Trinity*.

2. Ibid., xi.

3. Ibid., xix.

4. O'Mahony, *St. Thérèse of Lisieux by Those Who Knew Her*, 229.

5. Clarke, *General Correspondence, Vol. II*, 872.

6. Archives of the Carmel of Lisieux, "Circular of Sister Marie of the Trinity," https://www.archives-carmel-lisieux.fr/english/carmel/index.php/les-novices/marie-de-la-trinit%C3%A9/circulaire-de-marie-de-la-trinit%C3%A9.

7. O'Mahony, *St. Thérèse of Lisieux by Those Who Knew Her*, 249.

8. Descouvemont, *Thérèse of Lisieux and Marie of the Trinity*, xvii.

9. Ibid., 53.

10. Ibid., 41.

11. Archives of the Carmel of Lisieux, "Circular of Sister Marie of the Trinity."

12. Descouvemont, *Thérèse of Lisieux and Marie of the Trinity*, 64.

13. Ibid.

Chapter 12: Almire Pichon

1. Clarke, *Story of a Soul*, 149.

2. Ibid., 150.

Chapter 13: Maurice Bellière

1. Ahern, *Maurice and Thérèse*, 16.

2. Ibid., 3.

3. Ibid., 35–36. Maurice's biological mother, Marie Bellière, died shortly after his birth, prompting his father, Alphonse, to surrender him to his aunt, Antoinette Barthélémy, who raised him as her own.

4. Ibid., 271–273.

Chapter 14: Adolphe Roulland

1. Clarke, *General Correspondence, Vol. II*, 957.

2. Archives of the Carmel of Lisieux, "Witness 25: Adolphe Roulland," https://www.archives-carmel-lisieux.fr/english/carmel/index.php/25-adolphe-roulland.

Appendix B

1. Clarke, *General Correspondence, Vol. I*, 9 and 11.

Sources

Books

Ahern, Patrick. *Maurice and Thérèse: The Story of a Love.* New York, NY: Doubleday, 1998.

Chalon, Jean. *Thérèse of Lisieux: A Life of Love.* Liguori, MO: Liguori, 1997.

Clarke, OCD, John, trans. *General Correspondence, Vol. I.* Washington, DC: ICS Publications, 1982.

———. *General Correspondence, Vol. II.* Washington, DC: ICS Publications, 1988.

———. *St. Thérèse of Lisieux: Her Last Conversations.* Washington, DC: ICS Publications, 1977.

———. *Story of a Soul: The Autobiography of St. Thérèse of Lisieux.* Washington, DC: ICS Publications, 1975.

Day, Dorothy. *Thérèse.* Springfield, IL: Templegate, 1960.

Descouvemont, Pierre. *Thérèse of Lisieux and Marie of the Trinity: The Transformative Relationship of Saint Thérèse of Lisieux and Her Novice, Sister Marie of the Trinity.* Staten Island, NY: Alba House, 1997.

Gaucher, Guy. *The Passion of Thérèse of Lisieux.* New York, NY: Crossroad, 2000.

———. *The Story of a Life: St. Thérèse of Lisieux.* New York, NY: HarperCollins, 1987.

Görres, Ida Friederike. *The Hidden Face: A Study of St. Thérèse of Lisieux.* San Francisco, CA: Ignatius Press, 2003.

Kane, OCD, Aletheia, trans. *The Prayers of Saint Thérèse of Lisieux.* Washington, DC: ICS Publications, 1997.

Kinney, OCD, Donald, trans. *The Poetry of Saint Thérèse of Lisieux.* Washington, DC: ICS Publications, 1996.

Martin, SJ, James. *My Life with the Saints*. Chicago, IL: Loyola
    Press, 2006.
Miller, Frederick L. *The Trial of Faith of St. Thérèse of Lisieux*. Staten
    Island, NY: Alba House, 1998.
O'Connor, Patricia. *Thérèse of Lisieux: A Biography*. Huntington,
    IN: Our Sunday Visitor, 1983.
O'Mahony, OCD, Christopher, ed. and trans. *St. Thérèse of Lisieux
    by Those Who Knew Her: Testimonies from the Process of
    Beatification*. Dublin, IE: Veritas, 1975.
Tugwell, OP, Simon. *Ways of Imperfection: An Exploration of
    Christian Spirituality*. Springfield, IL: Templegate, 1985.

Online Sources

Academy of American Poets. https://poets.org.
Office Central de Lisieux. https://www.archives-carmel-lisieux.fr/
    english/carmel/.
Prendergast, Monica. "Found Poetry as Literature Review: Research
    Poems on Audience and Performance." *Qualitative
    Inquiry* 12, no. 2 (April 2006): 369–88. https://doi.
    org/10.1177/1077800405284601.

CPSIA information can be obtained
at www.ICGtesting.com
Printed in the USA
BVHW041345231121
622339BV00011B/438

9 781638 378853